THE DOCTOR IS IN

by
Maurice Berquist
with
**Illustrations by
Charles M. Schulz**

Published by
Warner Press, Inc.
Anderson, Indiana

i

Copyright © 1981 by Maurice Berquist
ISBN: 0-87162-253-X
All rights reserved
Printed in the United States of America
by Warner Press, Inc.,
Arlo F. Newell, editor in chief

To my wife, Berny, a devoted nurse
who has helped many broken bodies and minds
respond to the Doctor within

Contents

Hold on to your head. This is not just a book; this is a book to you—a conversation between me and you.

1

A Personal Confession to a Boy and His Dog

Charles Schulz sent me a book the other day. It is a great little book, full of pictures. Even more than the book itself, I love the handwritten note Mr. Schulz wrote on the flyleaf—a note to me written with a blue felt tip pen.

You understand, Charlie Brown, more than anyone, how I felt when I got that personal note from your creator. You keep looking at your mailbox for a letter—any kind of letter—especially a personal one.

I get so many form letters that look personal. Now computers even print my name in the letter to make me believe I am known. It's amazing, but no computer will ever replace the handwritten note from a friend.

So this is my personal letter to you, Charlie Brown. I love you. Millions of us love you. Your expressive face is the mirror in which we see ourselves every morning. When you look out of those little square boxes in the comic sections of our newspapers you are not only the mirror in which we see ourselves—you are the window through which we watch the rest of the world.

I know that this looks more like a book than a letter.

Frankly, it is a book—a book with covers and pictures. I had no choice, because when I started writing to you it turned out to be a long, long letter. Whom can I blame for that, Charlie Brown?

3

I'll blame you. If it weren't for you I wouldn't have this long list of questions rattling around in my mind. Now I am writing this letter to you.

It's still a personal letter—a letter to you. Can I help it if a few million people want to look over my shoulder as I write? If I simply wrote to you out there in Santa Rosa, California, all these people would still have their questions.

While I am confessing, I may as well say that books hold a special fascination for me. Books have helped to change the world. They have also helped to change my life.

Hold on to your head, Charlie Brown. This is not just a book; this is a book to you—a conversation, a confrontation between me and you.

The idea scares me.

Here I am, a grown man with enough wrinkles to prove that I have worried my way through battles I should never have fought. I ought to know better; I ought to avoid trouble. Then when I think that by talking back to you I am literally taking on the whole world, I wonder what has come over me.

It's a part of my job to put together a prime time nationwide television program that will talk to people about the things that make them unhappy—you know, things like loneliness, boredom, rejection, sickness, and guilt. I wanted to talk to them about discouragement and even despair that comes from these unanswered problems.

You know a lot about these things. After all, you are almost considered the patron saint of all of us who wait beside empty mailboxes.

Well, it isn't enough to talk about these things on a television program. I wanted to be certain that people would listen—and I wanted them to talk back.

That's how you got involved, Charlie Brown.

You and I know that your creator, Charles Schulz—or Sparky, as he likes his friends to call him—gets people to listen to him. Actually he speaks to more people every day than any other living human being.

One thousand seven hundred and thirty newspapers in America carry your story, Charlie Brown. Those little square boxes on the comic pages are the first windows through which a hundred million Americans look at the world each day. Even the president of the United States didn't feel he could start his occupancy in the White House without having read *Peanuts*.

I'm impressed. As a matter of fact, I'm almost speechless.

Just the other day I called Mr. George Pipals, who works with copyrights for all of you fabulous *Peanuts* people. His secretary said he was busy at the moment but would call me back as soon as he could. In a few hours he called.

"I'm sorry to be late returning your call, Maurice," he said, "but I have been busy all morning with the *Peanuts* repre-

5

sentative from Rome, Italy. I just now sent him to the plane to return."

"Now that we are talking about Rome, how is *Peanuts* doing in Italy?"

"There are 130 books about Charlie Brown in the Italian language," he said.

"Is that a world record?"

"Overseas, yes. But Japan is close behind. There are one hundred Charlie Brown titles in Japanese."

When I called Charles Schulz to ask if I could come to California to talk with him, I had no idea what an explosion would take place in my mind. I simply wanted to explore the idea of a book called *The Doctor Is In*. His illustrations would be immensely helpful if he would agree to let me use them.

Mr. Schulz agreed to talk with me.

What a day it was! I really didn't know what to expect as I walked up to the studio where he works.

Pat Lytle, one of the receptionists and secretaries, welcomed me and said, "Mr. Schulz will be down in a moment. Just sit down and make yourself comfortable."

How would you feel if you were sitting in the reception room of the world's most famous cartoonist and standing next to you (in fact, towering over you) was a stuffed Snoopy four feet tall?

I felt intimidated. So I got up and walked around the office. Covering much of one wall were framed magazine covers with you, Charlie Brown, on all of them. I forget all the names, but among them were *Life, Saturday Review, Woman's Day, Time,* and *Newsweek.* There was even a picture of Snoopy on his way to the moon.

Then I saw something that really made me feel at home. One wall was covered with framed cartoon strips, apparently some of Mr. Schulz's favorites. Many of them are my favorites, too.

There was one I particularly liked. In it, Charlie Brown, you are the star—the bewildered star, but the star.

6

NINE HOME RUNS IN A ROW!! GOOD GRIEF!

WHAT CAN I DO?!!

WE'RE GETTING SLAUGHTERED AGAIN, SCHROEDER.... I DON'T KNOW WHAT TO DO..WHY DO WE HAVE TO SUFFER LIKE THIS?

"MAN IS BORN TO TROUBLE AS THE SPARKS FLY UPWARD."

WHAT?

HE'S QUOTING FROM THE "BOOK OF JOB," CHARLIE BROWN... SEVENTH VERSE, FIFTH CHAPTER....

ACTUALLY, THE PROBLEM OF SUFFERING IS A VERY PROFOUND ONE, AND..

IF A PERSON HAS BAD LUCK, IT'S BECAUSE HE'S DONE SOMETHING WRONG, THAT'S WHAT I ALWAYS SAY!

THAT'S WHAT JOB'S FRIENDS TOLD HIM, BUT I DOUBT IF..

WHAT ABOUT JOB'S WIFE? I DON'T THINK SHE GETS ENOUGH CREDIT!

I THINK A PERSON WHO NEVER SUFFERS, NEVER MATURES...SUFFERING IS ACTUALLY VERY IMPORTANT..

WHO WANTS TO SUFFER? DON'T BE RIDICULOUS!

BUT PAIN IS A PART OF LIFE, AND..

A PERSON WHO SPEAKS ONLY OF THE "PATIENCE" OF JOB REVEALS THAT HE KNOWS VERY LITTLE OF THE BOOK! NOW, THE WAY I SEE IT...

I DON'T HAVE A BALL TEAM...I HAVE A THEOLOGICAL SEMINARY!

7

As I was looking at the cartoons, Mr. Schulz came down the short flight of stairs that leads to his "drawing room" and welcomed me. "Let's go upstairs and talk," he said.

Out of the corner of my eye I saw a jardiniere full of hockey sticks, a kind of sports-lover's bouquet. I learned that Schulz is an avid hockey fan. In fact, he plays hockey at the arena almost every week during the season.

The studio, or drawing room as I called it, is lined with books on art, theology, psychology, and a hundred other subjects.

When I finished my quick glance around the room, looking at the book titles and mementos of a life that ranges far and wide across our planet, I sat down and explained my purpose in coming.

"I am writing a book and putting together a television program that talks to people and encourages them to talk about the things that hurt them. Then I want to suggest some cures. I'd like to tell them that the Doctor is in."

Schulz said, "Well, I don't want to be a preacher or a moralizer."

"And I don't want you to," I answered.

"Cartoonists stand off and look at life," he continued. "They look at it a little sidelong—from a fresh angle or viewpoint. If they start explaining things or suggesting answers, people get tired of listening."

"I agree. But nobody seems to be tired of listening to you."

Frankly I had a whole hatful of questions I wanted to ask, but I didn't ask them. For example, I would like to have known if the name *Lucy* is not an abbreviation for *Lucifer,* one of the names of Satan.

I thought better of the idea. Probably Schulz just knew a girl named Lucy, so he decided to call the little dark-haired girl in the psychiatrist's booth Lucy.

There's probably a little bit of Lucy in all of us. We probably have Charlie Brown days, too, and top-of-the-doghouse Snoopy days and frustrating Peppermint Patty days and of course insecure days, just like Linus.

8

Fashions change in adult-model security blankets. But we are all looking for security; we just look in different places.

Let's face it, Charlie Brown, hundreds of millions of people relate to you and your *Peanuts* friends. You represent us all as Charles Schulz sits staring out the window of his California studio. You walk into his mind and ask the probing questions we all want to ask. In moments, these questions are flowing out from the point of Schulz's pen. Cartoons appear. They are mailed to New York to the syndicate offices and then they show up in newspapers all over the world. What I can't understand is why Snoopy gets all the fan mail.

You are in our papers, Charlie Brown, and in our hearts. Sorry we haven't written before. But this time the letter is for you, to thank you, to tell you we love you, and to find out more about that hope within you.

The Doctor is in. We are not alone.

Chapter 1
The World of Charlie Brown and Other Worriers
(Begin the Journey)

Charlie Brown, I know how you feel. When you are not thinking about how you got to this planet Earth, you are wondering why you came.

It's a little like a shipwrecked sailor swimming to land and then coming up all alone on an empty beach. It is a terrible feeling.

You obviously know the feeling—and the millions of people who read about you in scores of languages know the feeling, too. Rightfully, you are looking for a cure. I admire you for trying.

It's frightening—terrifying. We are thrust out into the world, as I say, like a shipwrecked sailor. Like Robinson Crusoe, we look around and think, What will I do if I get sick? As a matter of fact, what will I do if I stay well? Whom will I talk to? Am I truly alone?

There is not even a little psychiatrist's booth with a sarcastic dark-haired girl to promise us hope for another nickel. If you are truly alone even a sarcastic friend is better than no one.

Of course, that is not the best answer.

Answers come in all sizes and colors. When we think about the earth that is our home, we have to find out where we belong in it—and we have to find out if we are truly alone. How do we cope?

1. Admit it! We are all lonely.

We live "in between" lives. The Apostle Paul said it two thousand years before Lucy. "Now we see as through a dark and dirty window" (see 1 Corinthians 13:12). Life is like driving through an Indiana rainstorm, straining to see what lies ahead while squinting through the wet and terrifying darkness. The wheel is in my hands alone. I am steering. The choice to speed on, slow down, or stop under a friendly overpass and wait out the storm is mine. We are alone, and working out just how to live the in-between life is a lonely reality.

2. Even a best friend can't always help us escape the loneliness.

Oh, Charlie, you know how wonderful friends can be.

14

You are lucky. You have a whole gang of them. But even a roomful of friends will not help us escape the loneliness forever.

The mathematics of this is confusing. If you find another lonely person with whom you can share your loneliness, will you be half as lonely? Maybe! Unfortunately, you might become twice as lonely. Even two people standing together on the barren beach do not make a very big impression on the vast universe around them. Two people or four billion people are a very small part of the universe. Sometimes we even feel lonely in a crowd, and sharing that loneliness doesn't always help. You know that, Charlie Brown.

3. We may be lonely but we are not alone!

In Daniel Defoe's story *Robinson Crusoe,* when the ship-wrecked sailor landed safely on a desert island he first felt glad to be alive. Then, almost immediately, Crusoe felt sad and frightened to feel so alone.

So here it comes—the bias of this book: the Doctor is in. We are not alone. Of course, I cannot prove it. The answer is a matter of faith.

Naturally there are all kinds of hucksters who seem to forget that faith is still a very personal thing—even when it is shared with a friend. To return to the picture of the shipwrecked sailor on a lonely beach, we all must follow the footsteps in the sand for ourselves.

I like that about you, Charlie Brown. You have a wistfulness that charms me. Pushiness in faith rarely convinces anyone.

But there is no way to avoid the issue of faith. It can save your life to discover that you are not alone. What better news can there be than to learn that we live on a God-inhabited planet? This world belongs to him. He created it and he has plans for it and for each of us—personal plans. Now each of us is responsible to search for and follow the footprints of the Almighty, and to discover what he is like.

I know that's scary. Even Crusoe took a dangerous step when he began to follow the footprints in the sand. He couldn't know if they were the footprints of a potential friend or of a cannibal who would eat him. Following God's footprints is scary, too; but, like Crusoe, isn't it worth the risk to see if there really is someone there—to see if we are really not alone?

Go ahead. Start the journey. As you timidly follow the footprints in the sand they lead you to a path. Who made it? Where does it lead?

Now you begin to see signs of civilization. A garden has been carved out of the jungle. Precise and orderly rows of carrots, cabbages, and corn grow luxuriantly. This land belongs to someone who loves it.

Now you see a herd of cows in a fenced field. Who cares for them?

At last you see a house—or is it a palace?—gleaming in the sun. This land is ruled by a king. It is not a forgotten landmass in a nameless sea; it is a kingdom.

If the lord of this land is kind to the flowers and to the animals, will he be kind to you? If he cares for the fields, will he care for you?

You must find out.

Timidly you knock at the massive door of the gleaming palace. Your heart beats like a thousand drums as you wait.

To knock at the door of God is known as *prayer*.

Lucy is a little touchy about prayer, Charlie. Everybody is.

Even so, there is no other way to come to terms with the power behind this world—the kingdom of God. There, I have said it. That's the theme of this book—the kingdom of God. It is the world as God sees it, the world God wants us to have.

Can humor lead us to this kingdom? Can laughter, or tears?

Only through laughter may some people become relaxed enough to admit that they are secretly frightened by the prospect of living alone like unwelcome refugees on the planet Earth.

Truth about ourselves often comes as a gentle surprise; we are amused before we are amazed. I have to hand it to you, Charlie Brown, you get people to think about things that would ordinarily scare them to death. It's funny to watch you battle discouragement or ridicule. Only after I have put my newspaper aside and am slowly drinking my second cup of coffee do I realize you have shown me myself more clearly than the mirror before which I shaved a few moments earlier.

4. Jesus' footprints will lead us out of aloneness forever.

Listen to Jesus. Nobody tells us more about the kingdom of God than Jesus. He leads us gently into it.

What a fascinating experience it would be to listen to Jesus as he spoke! Stories would have flowed naturally in

17

the conversation. Simply calling them parables can scarcely conceal their charm. Conversation would have flowed easily without any chapter headings and Roman numerals. Smiles would not have been irreverent or flippant.

Jesus had this way. He talked about children and seeds, fish and fields, coins and vineyards. And he said, "The kingdom of God is like that." He never talked idly. His gentle storytelling slid into people's minds before they discovered he was not simply telling stories; he was diagnosing their sickness. And he was prescribing a cure.

Our defenses always seem to be up—even against things that are good for us.

In the world of *Peanuts,* Schroeder is convinced of the grandeur of Beethoven. He wishes everyone were. So he keeps playing his gentle song—and you know what happens!

For years Lucy screamed at Schroeder to play another song. But Schroeder continued to play the music of Beethoven until Beethoven broke through Lucy's defenses and she heard for the very first time those incredible harmonies, those luscious chords, those majestic crescendos.

God is very much like Schroeder. We ignore him. We pretend he isn't there. We laugh or jeer or curse at the very notion of his presence in this dark and lonely world. But God keeps playing his song of love until he breaks through our defenses and we hear him for the first time in our lives. He keeps teaching us until one day we see his footprints in the sand and turn to follow.

His prophets left their prints in the sand. For two thousand years they spoke clearly of his presence in the world. The footprints of martyrs and saints were stained in blood because they refused to give in and play another tune with their lives. Then Jesus came and walked among us. That's God himself leaving his footprints across the sands of time. And when we follow them, what a difference it can make! We are not sick people knocking helplessly on an abandoned hospital, dying because we are alone with no doctor to care for us. This is the good news. The Doctor is in. We are lonely but not alone. We are sick but there is someone who can heal us.

Even ancient prophets called by God to announce his presence in the world wondered from time to time if there really was a God and if he cared.

Chapter 2
Is There a Doctor in the House?
(What Happens If We Don't Begin the Journey?)

Sometimes it happens in an exciting basketball game. Above the shouting of the crowd and the feverish action of the players on the floor comes a sudden hush. A frantic voice has been heard over the loudspeakers: "Is there a doctor in the house?"

Sudden sickness has come. Perhaps a player has been more than slightly injured. Perhaps a person in the audience is the sudden victim of a stroke or heart attack. Help is needed.

In those electric moments the crowd goes silent. People whisper nervously as they look in all directions, hoping to see someone respond. The attitude is almost prayerful.

The cry "Is there a doctor in the house?" is an ancient one, We hear it in the voice of Jeremiah the prophet:

For the wound of . . . my people is my heart wounded,
I mourn, and dismay has taken hold on me.
Is there no balm in Gilead?
Is there no physician there?
Why then has the health of . . . my people
Not been restored?

—Jeremiah 8:21-22

Charlie, even ancient prophets called by God to announce his presence in the world wondered from time to time if there really was a God and if he really cared about his world—about people. There is plenty of evidence that if there is a God he certainly doesn't care. We are surrounded by war, famine, disease, injustice, inequality, and death. It is easy to give in to the terror, to quit hoping there is a loving God, to quit believing that the Doctor is in. But when you give up the journey toward him, when you quit looking for his footprint in the sand and wander off alone in the desert, certain results are guaranteed. You get lost—lost and lonely.

Charlie Brown, you are especially wonderful at helping us remember the awful, lonely results of unbelief.

What happens if we give up—or maybe don't even start?

1. Go on feeling unhappy.

Why is it that just when we feel happy something always comes to spoil it? Why almost every time we have happiness in our grasp does something steal it away again? Happiness is a glistening bubble—when we touch it, it disappears. Charlie, you know how it is, but do you know why? Both believers and nonbelievers experience happiness. People of every race, color, and creed find it in an infant's birth, in a child's first steps, in the first kiss of two young lovers, in a wedding feast, in music, and in food and friends. But then, with the smile still on our faces, the music still ringing in our ears, something always happens to change the scene of life and laughter to tragedy and sorrow once again.

The infant is born with a cleft palate, the child is struck down by a drunken driver, the two young lovers quarrel and the wedding feast ends in a divorce court, the music grows dissonant, the friends die or disappear and we are alone again. Without belief, when those awful, real moments of unhappiness reappear, we have no solid ground on which to stand, no place to flee for refuge, no Person at the center of the universe to hold us and give us comfort, no joy to keep us through the long unhappy nights.

Belief, on the other hand, is remembering history's greatest headline. God has good news for his wandering planet

Earth. Remember? Angels fluttered white wings against the blue Judean sky over the grazing lands of Bethlehem. The startled shepherds could scarcely believe their eyes and ears!

"Behold, I bring you good tidings of great *joy* which shall be to all people. For unto you is born this day in the city of David a Savior, which is Christ the Lord."

Great joy. Is it possible that the stern God whose name had been thought too sacred to be pronounced by a human tongue is now smiling? Was his greatest gift to his wayward planet to be wrapped with light and called joy?

Who forgot to tell us? Maybe it is simply that the dust of the centuries has settled on all the stories about Jesus. Perhaps it is a deliberate deception by an imp with infernal indigestion. For whatever reason, the truth has been garbled. To believe and to follow God's steps is to find joy that keeps us through those unhappy times. To refuse to believe, to give up the journey after him, is to go on being unhappy forever.

2. Go on feeling guilty.

Guilt, Charlie Brown, can lead to nervous tension, ulcers, sickness, even death. Or guilt can lead us to forgiveness and new beginnings. Doctors say so much of what ails us comes from guilt we carry secretly down inside us. It may be something we said to or about a person that hurt or was untrue, something we stole from a neighbor, or something we did that took advantage of another person's weakness. It is in the very heart of God's creation that any thought or act that was destructive or dehumanizing must be forgiven or it will haunt us forever. The wrong can be toward God or toward our neighbor. Guilt is that wonderful gift from God, that reminder that something needs to be done to put away the wrong forever and begin new and clean again. But guilt that isn't taken care of may haunt and destroy us.

To believe that there is a God who is alive and willing to forgive us, to believe that same God can give us strength to ask forgiveness from our friends and neighbors means guilt can no longer be our master. Guilt will never cripple us again.

But to refuse to believe that the Doctor is in, that there is a God who can forgive us, is to go on being unforgiven for those acts and means that guilt will forever destroy us.

3. Go on feeling dread.

Two thousand years before you said it, Charlie, Jesus said it another way: "Sufficient unto the day is the evil thereof" (Matt. 6:34). Every new day is packed full of potential tragedy. The threat of war hangs over our heads like a yellow cloud of smog. Nuclear holocaust, terrorism, economic chaos, and international tragedy threaten us continually. Goodness—AAUGH!—it is easier to narrow down our dread to one day at a time, but without belief there is no hope that dread will ever give way to peace again. Always living under a cloud of dread will cripple us. Believing that there is a Creator and that he is in charge of the universe and that he will see us through these dread-filled days is the only way we can bear the pressure and not be crushed by it. To refuse to believe, to go on fearing that there is no sense in this life and no guarantee of life to come is to be destroyed by dread even if we follow your advice, Charlie, and dread only one day at a time.

4. Go on being sick.

So we suffer from unforgiven guilt. So we go down slowly under each day's accumulating dread. At least we know the problems and, though crippled by them, we prefer what we know to what is unknown to us. We would rather stay sick in the waiting room than take that walk into the doctor's examination office with its powders, potions, and pills and its knives, razors, and needles all in a row. It is normal to fear what will happen next when the doctor is in, whether it's our medical doctor working on our physical illness or the Lord of all creation working on our soul.

So we are asking for help. We are facing some new questions.

What if the Doctor is incompetent?

When we read the medical history of a little more than a century ago we are horrified. It was a common practice for surgeons to wipe their hands on their aprons as they operated on a patient. Strange as it seems, they came to pride themselves on their bloodstained aprons and trousers. To wear a spotless apron was almost an advertisement of the doctor's lack of popularity.

We cringe at this—and we should. Modern symbols of surgical success are often exotic foreign automobiles and lavish homes. These things let people know that the doctor is well respected. But Mercedes sport coupes or bloody aprons can't guarantee that we can trust the doctor.

How can we decide between one religion and another? Whose God will really be competent to help us? Whose church should we attend? How can we be sure? It's all so complex that we give up and stay sick. But one day we have to decide, to take a risk, to leave the safety of the sickness that is killing us and place our lives in the hands of the Doctor who is in.

There's nothing wrong with getting more than one medical opinion before you decide between an operation and a series of radiation treatments or chemicals taken by mouth. So look around before you decide. Compare Jesus with all the other religious options. Then decide.

What if the Doctor is a phoney?

For one brief uncaptioned moment, Charlie, you stand staring at the doctor. You can hear your brain whirling in that almost round head of yours: That's no doctor. That's my dog. Still you sat down to counsel with Snoopy, knowing he probably couldn't help you.

But he has such a warm nose and friendly face, you think. He would be hurt if I walked away. I would be embarrassed to reject him.

How easily we give ourselves up to the sellers of religion on television or to local cult leaders. Jim Jones took over one thousand of our neighbors to Jonestown and then killed them. Nine million of our fellow Americans belong to cults today as though Jonestown had never happened.

So we can give in to the phonies. We can refuse to search for the authentic in and among the phonies. Or we can carefully search and decide.

What if the Doctor is too busy for my little problems?

For a moment, Charlie, you were made to feel important. That unseen nurse looked down her nose at you like Jesus' disciples looked down their noses at the children to send them away. Remember what Jesus said, "Let the children come unto me. Don't stop them. For they are of the kingdom of heaven" (see Matthew 19:14).

We are all children, Charlie. We all feel that our problems are too little for the Creator of the world to care about.

But when you follow Jesus' steps, you'll find them surrounded by children's footprints in the sand. If he cared so much about them and about their common fisherman fathers and homemaking moms, about the poor and the dirty and the sick and the old, he will care about you.

The most reassuring fact of the universe is that the Doctor is in. He is concerned not only about the galaxies but about the flowers of the field and the people who get hay fever from them.

What if the Doctor is too small for my big problems?

One of the most comforting things about having faith in God as the Great Physician is his attention to what seem to be insignificant details: "Consider the lilies of the field," said Jesus. "They neither toil nor spin, yet . . . Solomon in all his glory was not arrayed like one of these. But if God so clothes the grass of the field, which today is alive and tomorrow is thrown into the oven, will he not much more clothe you?" (Matt. 6:29-30).

Think about it. The "Doctor who is in" created this whole

universe, yet stoops to straighten the petals of a daisy. It shouldn't be hard to trust him with our cares.

I remember calling a piano tuner to get our piano fixed. It was sadly out of tune. The piano tuner was philosophic about it. "People don't have their pianos tuned because the piano needs it; they have them tuned because they can't stand it."

Excuses, excuses. How easy it is to put off seeing the Doctor who is in. Then how quickly comes the day when it is too late. Then we start hoping for a miracle to get us out of the predicament our own wishy-washiness got us into.

For a moment your dog sat dumbly in the rain waiting for a rich lady in a big car, a miracle cure, a fantasy. Then he did what he should have done all along. He quit feeling sorry for himself, picked himself off the ground, and started home.

Charlie, do you remember that young man who took his share of the family wealth, wasted it in a far country, and ended up eating with the pigs and feeling sorry for himself? That young man turned around and walked the road back to his father's house. He quit making excuses. And his father was there on the road, arms outstretched waiting for him.

Night after night we lie on top of our own doghouses or in our favorite watering spots and wonder why we were born.

Chapter 3
What's a Nice Person Like Me Doing in a Place Like This? (Consider the Evidences That the Doctor Is In)

Poor Snoopy! He didn't ask to be born either. One day he just woke up at the Daisy Hill Puppy Farm in a squirming, squealing litter of newborn pups. Now he will spend this lifetime—with the rest of us—wondering why.

Some of us never get beyond that question. Night after night we lie on top of our own doghouses or in our favorite watering spots and wonder why we were born. After another evening's frustration, we throw up our hands, confess the question is beyond our comprehension, and quit wondering for another day.

But here and there people climb down off their indecision and begin the search. That's what this chapter is about. I believe there are answers to Snoopy's questions: Why was I born? Why was I put here on this earth? What am I doing here? And the answers begin with an even more difficult question—the question this book seeks to answer: Is the Doctor in? Is there a loving Creator behind creation who still walks among us, and who lives and moves and acts in our lives and through our lives? Or are we chance accidents of a mechanical, evolutionary process?

Once that question is answered, once you join in confessing that the Doctor is in, once you have settled that there is a powerful God who never stops loving us and working for our good, it's easy to answer those other questions: Why was I born and why do I now live on planet Earth?

The Natural Proofs

We start with the proofs found in creation all about us. Oh, there are no proofs in the sense of logic or mathematics. I cannot prove to you without a shadow of doubt that God is or that God created and loves you. But the evidences accumulate. All I can hope is that as you sift through the evidences of all kinds, they will become sufficient to help you believe in him. One place to begin is the created universe about us.

The psalmist says, "The heavens are telling the glory of God; and the [earth] proclaims his handiwork" (Ps. 19:1). Linus says it in quite another way.

36

Your friend Linus has many talents, Charlie. He can even catch a softball and quote from the ancient Old Testament Book of Job. He's using the Creation as proof of the existence of a loving Creator. Like a multi-media show, Linus flashes amazing pictures past you, Charlie. You see

37

pictures of the day the world was created and the night billions of stars began their journey through the sky. He asks if you could explain the origin of the sea or the mystery of snow and rain and storm clouds whirling overhead. He reminds you of the wonders of the animal world. You can see the oxen that pulled the plows and the horses that carried our ancestors across the wilderness. Linus, in a sentence, sends hawks soaring across the heavens in a mystery of migration.

Like Job you were about to give up on creation, Charlie, just because you felt hot and sweaty. But Linus, with the wisdom of a Little League catcher calming his overheated pitcher on the mound, reminds you that nature and all its wonders point to a Creator who will see us through those miserable days.

Sure we have miserable moments when nature goes berserk. There are hurricanes, earthquakes, fires, and floods. Insurance adjusters call them "acts of God" as though creation is capricious and occasionally sends out natural horrors to torment us. Science can explain most of these natural disasters. Tides flood the land of India where people build too close to the sea. Fires have regularly swept through the California foothills from the beginning of time to clean off the brush and refertilize the land. But people today build their homes in those same ancient canyons and scream out at God when their homes burn or their families die.

Who can understand disasters even with these natural explanations? When lightning strikes a child—especially our own child—we must decide about the Doctor who is in all over again. Even in tragedy is it better to believe there is no God, that creation is an accident, and that we are results of a creatorless bang? Or can the loving, caring God still be seen in the order and the beauty and the rule of the universe?

The Supernatural Proofs

Imagine it. In the Bible there are sixty-six different books, written over a period of thousands of years by some forty

38

different authors. But it is not the Bible that is supernatural. Real people wrote those letters that Linus is embarrassed to read. And those real writers tell a tale that shocked and surprised them as much as it shocks and surprises us. It is the supernatural story of God at work creating a perfect world and giving at the same time freedom to his creation to build or to destroy, to give life or give death. And when in the earliest days those same people chose to disobey him, it is the story of God's supernatural acts to redeem his creation from their own destruction.

Consider the evidence of the Children of Israel in slavery in Egypt and their supernatural deliverance from pharaoh's armies. Consider the evidence of that tiny band of ex-slaves wandering for forty years across the desert and the cloud by day and the fire by night that led them to the land God promised. Consider the evidence of Joshua and the walls of Jericho being supernaturally razed to the ground. Consider the supernatural evidences of Daniel in the lion's den, of Samson beside the pillars of the Philistine banquet hall, of David before Goliath, of Peter and the lame man who was healed, of Stephen dying in a hail of stones, and from Stephen's blood the conversion of the Apostle Paul. Consider the supernatural evidence of Jesus' life, death, and resurrection, and of God's Spirit descending on a band of frightened cowards and transforming them into an army of love that toppled the pagan Roman Empire. Consider these and ask yourself, What does it mean to me?

As the evidences pile up we begin to believe, and as we believe we are not alone anymore. That takes a great load off our minds and makes us free to quit stumbling about in unbelief and confusion and get on with the task of following God to where he wants to lead us.

The Human Proofs

Unfortunately, the newspaper all too often provides evidence that people are an accident. The evidence shows that they are in fact worse than animals in their dealings with other people. The police blotters that trace crime in our

39

cities every day stagger the imagination with their growing catalog of rape, robbery, and murder. Those who choose not to believe point to the headlines with their daily stories of terrorism and assassination and nuclear war, of the burnings and bombings and bayonetings, and ask, What human proof is there of a loving God behind creation?

Charlie Brown, you know how bad it is out there. Like each of us you have experienced cruelty not just from enemies but from your friends as well.

The Bible clearly tells us that humankind is not living up to God's dream. And the newspapers go on to prove it in every generation. But now and then the spark of what God had in mind for us shines through and we see it glimmering there and think of him.

When we discover that there is something in us that won't let us accept the idea we are nothing—that's really something, or someone!

But other times, people can reach out to us in ways that change our lives forever, or at least they turn a miserable moment into a moment of joy. Those moments point to God and add to that pile of evidence for a loving Creator behind creation.

The Personal Proof

Sometimes it backfires to be reminded that each of us is special, that each of us can make a difference to the world no matter how small it seems to us. And people can use our "potential" to trigger guilt in us. But soon enough we will realize again that we are special.

That, too, is a kind of evidence that we are not simply accidents. We are created by a loving God who has plans for each of us. Sometimes we get so far from those plans. Sometimes it's so hard to think we have any talent, any future, any value at all. But at other times, we hear his voice quietly calling us to follow. For most of us there has been no voice from a burning bush, no handwriting on the wall, no angel visitors with a singing telegram from the Creator. But there are moments when we feel it. Better yet, there are moments when we feel him inside us reminding us he loves us and has a great dream for us. Haven't you felt it? Isn't that also evidence that he exists and that we should take the risk and believe in him?

41

There are evidences, Charlie Brown, that even your life can make a difference. And when I watch you smile, I remember those times in my own life when tears of grief or joy have filled my eyes. I remember those moments and somehow they remind me that the Doctor is in. And through my tears, I see God standing there and realize I am not alone.

Running away may unite us on one path, but what kind of solution is that?

Chapter 4

Things You Hear in the Doctor's Waiting Room (Refusing to Enter the Kingdom)

You can spend only so much valuable time in the agony of disbelief. You must decide sometime. Is there a Creator who loves me or is there not? There will never be enough evidences for proving it one way or the other. But when you get enough evidences in your pile to make the choice, make it. Unfortunately, some people spend their lifetimes searching but never deciding. They are, as Paul once suggested, always looking for the truth but never coming to it. In this chapter, we will look at some of the typical ways people avoid making a decision about God.

1. We can run away from the evidence altogether.

This task of seriously deciding if there is a God or not can be a scary process, too. Everybody tells us something different. There are so many evidences for and against the possibility of a loving God still at work in the world today. And even if there is a God there are so many conflicting paths to him. Linus has a solution:

Running away may unite us on one path, but what kind of solution is that? Besides, the psalmist says wherever we run, God will be there running after us. Listen to a paraphrase of his words from Psalm 139:

Tho I flee to the bottom of the Sea
Thou art there.
Tho I take the wings of the morning
And fly above the clouds
Your spirit seeks for me.
In the dark of the forest deep
Or on waves of desert sand
You are with me, God
And you will find me.

2. We can cut short our search in fear and frustration.

46

Let's face it. We're all afraid. It isn't easy to decide which sandwich you want at McDonald's, let alone make these gigantic lifetime decisions. So we grow frustrated and afraid. Fear immobilizes. Fear becomes a kind of choice, and once we settle into it fear can dominate and destroy us.

Stockbrokers who succeed are those who can make careful decisions quickly and when they realize they've made a mistake cut their losses and move on. Perhaps it's an inappropriate example to compare the search for God to the person in the marketplace who must make and live with difficult decisions everyday, but it is something to consider, nevertheless. It may be better to make a decision that is wrong and then to pay the price and get out than to go on undecided forever. And what about the in-between times? Try Snoopy's remedy:

I don't know what it proves either, Snoopy, but I am sure that somehow after howling at the moon you feel better. The Greeks called it *catharsis*. My mother called it having a good old-fashioned two-hankie cry. Psychologists call it the primal scream. When our fear and our frustration reach the limit, maybe a good howl at the moon would help us. But when our tears are dried and our mind is clear again, then it is important to make the decision and get on with it.

3. *We could laugh off the entire process as unimportant.* So many people see this quest for God as an ancient ritual outdated by the age of science and space travel. They watch television evangelists. They read stories of the cults. They get books pressed into their hands on street corners and in airports by overzealous Christian youth out to "save them." They see Catholic Christians in Ireland fighting the Protestant Christians who live next door. Cynicism sets in. The search ends.

It is dangerous to confuse the mass of religious options with the still, small voice of God. It may be confusing. It may be difficult to decide. Not one of God's representatives is perfect. We're all human. Yes, I admit we believers have occasional fights on our church boards. Yes, I admit we sometimes act like children and sulk and take our toys and refuse to play. Yes, I admit that none of us is really like God. The bumper sticker says it perfectly. You've read it: "Christians Are Not Perfect, Just Forgiven." Don't quit searching for him because of us. We're no excuse.

4. *We can retreat into a fantasy world and wait until everything is perfect before we decide or dream that some-one wonderful will come along to decide for us.*

For Peppermint Patty it is simpler to dream of a scholarship to Vassar than to sit through her fourth-grade lecture on English grammar. "Well, back to reality," she says, straightening up and raring to go. The dream is over. The work begins again. Beware dreaming that it can be simple. Beware hoping for a new messiah that will make it easy. Beware searching for someone who will tell you what to believe and how. Beware turning your lives over to anybody. That dream can become a nightmare. Ask those who survived the Jonestown tragedy. They can tell you.

Weighing the evidences for and against belief can be a difficult and demanding process. Some people are gifted with simple faith. For others it is a lifelong quest. A military leader with a mind for complex strategy and logic met Jesus one day almost two thousand years ago and said it best. "Lord, I believe; help thou mine unbelief" (Mark 9:24).

5. We can give in to doubt and stop our search altogether.

This is a moment when so many of our friends and neighbors have given up the search and settled into lives of work and pleasure with no thought for the eternal realities. Make a buck; enjoy the moment; and die. Why go on wondering about God? He'll only crimp your style anyway if you find him.

Charlie, you know how it feels to have someone make you doubt yourself. But in reality we are our own worst enemies in the doubt department. We worry that we aren't smart enough or well-read enough. We wonder if we know enough or have studied enough. We wonder and we doubt and we worry. There is very little time for doubting. Read the Gospels (Matthew, Mark, Luke, and John). Jesus walked up to perfect strangers and said, "Follow me." He didn't say that the way ahead would be free of doubts. He just said to begin the journey and the doubts would take care of themselves along the way.

But don't be afraid if you are doubting. Jesus loved doubters. Look at Thomas. Even after the Resurrection, after they saw him die and then appear mysteriously in his risen body in their presence, Thomas doubted. Jesus, rather than rejecting the doubter, simply reached out, took Thomas' hand, and placed it on the wounds in his hands and side. Doubt! Question! Seek! Remember Jesus' words, "Seek, and you will find" (Matt. 7:7). There's nothing wrong with having questions and getting them answered, but let your doubting be the beginning and not the end of the process.

6. We can discuss it and never decide.

We believers spend a lot of time talking things to death. Nonbelievers are the same. It seems almost holy to talk about religious matters. Discussion becomes not a way of finding the truth but of avoiding it altogether. Righteousness is lost in rhetoric, decision is discussion, and truth in talk.

Someone has observed that a committee is a group of

people who cannot do anything individually and who meet together to decide that nothing can be done.

Jesus said, "If any man will do [God's] will, he shall know of the doctrine" (John 7:17).

Again, "Not every one who says to me, 'Lord, Lord,' shall enter the kingdom of heaven but he who does the will of my Father" (Matt. 7:21).

Truthfully, the parts of the Bible that disturb us are not the parts that we cannot understand; they are the parts we do understand and find difficult to obey. They confront us.

In the matter of the kingdom of God, which we have discussed throughout this book, we are confronted by Christ's powerful announcements—and by his invitation to "seek first the Kingdom."

Try it! Seeking first his kingdom can be the beginning of the greatest adventure ever. Besides, if you haven't decided to follow him, you've in fact decided against doing so. You can't really have it both ways. Not to decide is to decide.

The guilt we have long since talked
ourselves out of is God's voice inside
us leading us gently back to himself.

Chapter 5
We Are Made for Each Other
(Respond and Enter the Kingdom)

L inus spent three of the preceding cartoon sequences giving positive thinking his best try. Then he gave it up and walked quickly out of the rain. It is impossible to positive-think your way out of a rainstorm or into the kingdom of God. Once you have considered the evidences and found them sufficient to believe, there is an ancient, biblically based process that everyone who wishes to enter the kingdom of God must follow.

You cannot inherit the Kingdom like a piece of land or an heirloom. You cannot join the Kingdom like you join a gym or country club. You cannot buy it and add it to the things you own. You cannot be born into the Kingdom as you are born into a race or nation or social stratum. Don't worry! Entering the Kingdom is not complex. It is not difficult. But it is a process; and though various Christian traditions may name the process differently, in essence the path to God has not changed in two thousand years. There is only one way: Jesus' way!

Picture it. The Master is hurrying along a dark, cobble-stone street late one evening in Palestine. Suddenly out of the shadows emerges a wealthy and powerful young politician. Nicodemus had been considering carefully the evidences for and against the possibility that this Jesus really was the promised Messiah. He had to know for sure one way or the other. False messiahs had been making claims for centuries. Churchly tribunals had ignored some and had tried, punished, and even executed others. Few, if any, were treated seriously, especially by the elite—and Nicodemus was a member of the elite.

The young man was probably embarrassed to be seen talking with Jesus. It was beneath his dignity to talk to an itinerant Galilean peasant teacher. But something about this man made Nicodemus curious. And so he came to Jesus by night, hidden by the shadows, and was faced by a decision each of us must make.

Nicodemus: "Rabbi, we know that thou art a teacher come from God: for no man can do these

> miracles that thou doest, except God be with him."
>
> Jesus: "I say unto thee, Except a man be born again, he cannot see the kingdom of God" (John 3:1-3).

Ooops. There it is. The phrase on the cover of *Time* and *Newsweek;* the phrase used to brand politicians and electric preachers; the phrase bandied about on books and banners, revival meetings, and talk shows. You must be *born again.* It's old hat now—even commonplace. The phrase is a buzz word, an epithet, a label to revere or caricature, a bumper sticker. But that night it was new and Nicodemus staggered into the light with a growing look of unbelief on his face.

> Nicodemus: "How can a man be born when he is old?"
>
> Jesus: "I say unto thee, Except a man be born of water [natural birth] and of the Spirit [spiritual birth], he cannot enter the kingdom of God" (John 3:4-5).

For a moment they talked in whispers and then Jesus was gone. For a heartbeat Nicodemus stood hypnotized by the encounter, then he hurried through the darkness to his home. That bright young man must have been terribly troubled as Jesus' words echoed in his brain.

> Jesus: "For God so loved the world, that he gave his only begotten Son, that whosoever believeth in him should not perish, but have everlasting life. For God sent not his Son into the world to condemn the world; but that the world through him might be saved. He that believeth on him is not condemned: but he that believeth not is condemned already" (John 3:16-18).

Inevitably all the evidence in our search for truth about God will lead to Jesus. And if you take him seriously—if you find him a man of honor who can be trusted—then you cannot, as Nicodemus could not, ignore his claim about himself. Jesus is at the heart of the process for entering into the kingdom of God. When you decide about Jesus you decide about God. How did Nicodemus' story end? We aren't sure.

Nicodemus' name is mentioned only twice more in all of biblical literature. In the Sanhedrin (supreme court and congress) in Jerusalem, Nicodemus spoke on Jesus' behalf. "Doth our law judge any man, before it hear him, and know what he doeth?" (John 7:51). But the leaders stared Nicodemus down with the question "Are you also from Galilee?" They were saying, "What are you, a hick like Jesus?"

The last time we hear Nicodemus' name is in a rather tragic but ambiguous reference. Again, John on the scene reports what happened. Jesus was dead. His friends were about to bury him in a borrowed tomb. Suddenly into the cemetery comes Nicodemus with a hundred pounds of expensive spices to anoint the Master's body (see John 19:39).

History will never be sure if this was the last loving act of one who considered the evidence, believed, and was born again, or the last tragic act in the life of a man who came close but could not decide.

1. You'll Never Be Good Enough. Confess It!

"All have sinned, and come short of the glory of God" (Rom. 3:23).

We are no different from each other. Each of us is greedy. Each of us has sinned. Each has fallen short of God's dream for us. Each of us has failed. Unfortunately, each of us does not feel guilty, Charlie. Again, you lead us toward health. The guilt we have long since talked ourselves out of, rationalized away, is God's voice inside us leading us gently back to himself.

58

Apparently, there is nothing we can do to be good enough to enter the Kingdom on our own good works. Charlie, you know the only thing we can do is quit double-talking, making excuses, and pretending to be good when inside we know the truth of our sinfulness. You know our only option is to throw ourselves on the mercy of the court.

"If we confess our sins, he is faithful and just to forgive us our sins and to cleanse us from all unrighteousness" (1 John 1:9).

Perhaps you will kneel or have knelt at the high altar of a great city cathedral or on a rough mourner's bench in an Appalachian camp meeting. Perhaps you have spoken your confession to a priest or pastor in a church office or pew or to a dad or mom in your bedroom or around the dining room table or alone to God crumpled over a steering wheel in despair or beside a beautiful stream.

It doesn't matter where or when you confess. It doesn't matter if you are alone or with somebody. What matters is that you realize your sinfulness and confess it to the loving God who is there to forgive. He will begin in you a wonderful lifelong process and give you a place forever in his kingdom.

2. New Life Is Free. Accept It!

"The wages of sin is death; but the gift of God is eternal life through Jesus Christ our Lord" (Rom. 6:23).

"By grace are ye saved through faith . . . It is a gift of God: not of works, lest any man should boast" (Eph. 2:8-9).

The gift of salvation is free to us but it cost God everything. He paid for our sins by dying on that rugged Roman instrument of torture and death. He volunteered to pay with his life for our eternal lives. Don't ask me how it works. Don't ask me how God could pay with his life the penalty justice demanded of him. Don't ask me to explain how Christ's life, death, and resurrection works. I don't understand it. I just believe it is true. His word tells me it's true. The history of the Church verifies its effectiveness. And I have found it true in my own life and experience.

Now, when I hear a black choir sing "Amazing Grace" or hear it played on a great ten-rank pipe organ in St. John's Cathedral or hear the children sing it around a campfire or on a bus trip, I want to stand up and shout for joy. I spent so many years trying to earn my way into God's favor. And then one day I learned it was his free gift to me. "I'll take it!" I shouted, and I have been shouting gratefully ever since. Day after day I love to hear him say it again. "Take it. It is free. I love you!"

3. We Need Each Other. Admit It!

"[Do not forsake] the assembling of [yourselves] together" (Heb. 10:25).

"And they continued stedfastly in the apostles' doctrine and fellowship, and in breaking of bread and in prayers" (Acts 2:42).

Through your confession and God's free gift in Christ you have entered an entirely new world: the kingdom or dominion or people of God. You have new brothers and sisters in Christ. You have new ancestors reaching back to Moses, Paul, Luther, Bonhoeffer, and King. You have new brothers and sisters in Christ who are Baptists and Catholics and Presbyterians. Those brothers and sisters are black and red and yellow and white. They live in Cairo and Mexico City and Vladivostok.

That's what the Church is: brothers and sisters in Christ past and present, dead and living. And you will need them all, for the Kingdom is a lifelong adventure. We know so little when we begin. We cannot make the journey alone. Christ is no longer with us in the flesh, so he left his new spiritual body, the Church, to put its arm around us when we stumble. He left the Church to hold us tight when we feel afraid, to wipe away our tears when they just won't stop falling, to laugh with us and cry with us and sing his praises with us. Through the Church he confronts us when we get off track, questions us when we need it, and loves us in silence and understanding when we are unwilling to love.

I love that cartoon, Charlie, in which your little sister tells you that she wants to learn all about religion—"about Moses and St. Paul and Minneapolis." I love your stunned look as you echo, "Minneapolis?" She needs you, Charlie, as I need my brothers and sisters in Christ.

61

Your little sister needs you, Charlie, and Linus needs you and I need you. I suppose that's what is so wonderful about your *Peanuts* gang. With all the words that fly between you, the ups and downs in relationships, the anger and the laughter, the wins and the losses, the summers and the winters—with all of that you need each other.

And we who are brothers and sisters in Christ, kingdom kids, patients of the Doctor who is in, we need each other, too. Don't listen to all the critics of the Church. It's true we who make up his body may fight and argue. We call one another heretics and hypocrites now and then. But without one another we could not survive. Join us. We aren't perfect, but until you take your place in a local cell of that great growing body of Christ, you risk losing what God has begun in you.

4. The Kingdom Brings Peace. Enjoy It!

"Peace I leave with you; my peace I give to you; not as the world gives do I give you. Let not your hearts be troubled, neither let them be afraid" (John 14:27).

How often when we enter the Kingdom we take all of our fears and our frustrations with us. I spent so much of my own Christian life working too hard for the Kingdom in my traveling, preaching, and writing. But all God wants of me is to love him and enjoy him forever.

Don't worry, our brothers and sisters will give us the guilts if we let them. There's always one more job to be done at church, one more project to be accomplished, one more person in the neighborhood who needs my help, one more unbeliever who needs my presence. And so we begin to run faster and faster, until there is no longer time to sit on that bench and wait for God to meet us there. To feel God's presence takes time. Our overactive brain needs turning down. Our busy lives take time to refocus. To enjoy my brothers and sisters in the Body may mean taking time off from projects we are working on and just being together under a tree or sitting in the grass

There is new peace when you enter the Kingdom. Your past is forgiven. Your future is secure. Your present is in his hands. Now take some time each day simply to relax and enjoy that peace.

5. *The Good News Is for Everyone. Share It!*

"I was hungry and you gave me food, I was thirsty and you gave me drink, I was a stranger and you welcomed me, I was naked and you clothed me, I was sick and you visited me. I was in prison and you came to me . . . Truly, I say to you, as you did it to one of the least of these you did it to me" (Matt. 25:35-40).

"Go therefore and make disciples of all nations, baptizing them in the name of the Father and of the Son and of the Holy Spirit, teaching them to observe all that I have commanded you" (Matt. 28:19-20).

That's it, Charlie Brown, that is our dilemma—yours and mine. We are here to relax and enjoy the Father. We are also here to do our Father's business. Walking that tightrope is a lifelong task. We are not in the Kingdom just to relax. We are called to work and to witness, and keeping the two in balance is no easy job.

Every day kingdom dwellers awaken to those choices once again. Every day enough people with needs stumble through our lives to keep us busy forever. God loves everyone of those people and wants his best for them. At the same time we have limits. We have limited resources, limited energy, limited time. He knows that and he understands. Lovingly, he leaves us with very difficult choices. But remember, everything we do for them we are doing for him. Our work in the Kingdom flows not from guilt and fear but out of our love for God.

Sometimes when we reach out in his name our efforts will

look silly and halfhearted and unproductive. Other times we will succeed and lives will be changed. My goal is that one day, God will reach out to me and say, "Nice try, Berk. You did what you could and I'm proud of you."

In the meantime, I am glad and grateful that he loves me, forgives me, and continues working in and through my life, whether I fail or succeed as a worker and as a witness for the Kingdom.

When we accept the family relation-ship in the kingdom of God, we don't need to apologize for our decision. We are truly special.

Chapter 6
The Morning After:
Dealing with My New Self

Charlie, your morning-after look fits the theme of this chapter perfectly. We go to bed the night before having decided that the Doctor is in, and that we will begin a new life in Christ. Then we wake up the next morning feeling that nothing has really changed at all. That is a dangerous moment. Belief is fragile. The first tiny blade that belief sends up through the dirt can be crushed on that awful *morning after* when reality comes crashing down to bend and break and bury it again.

So what can we do on the morning after and the morning after that and the morning after that to help belief grow and flower and bear fruit? I want to suggest a simple exercise. Before your feet hit the floor, before you rush to the bathroom, before you throw on clothes and gag down breakfast and run out the door to school or work, there are some short sentence prayers I'd like you to pray. Read them every day this week. Next week they should be automatic and in your own words. But this week read them. Becoming a Christian may not seem to change the everyday world you live in, at least not right away. But pray these prayers. Let the truth in each of them grow in you and little by little something wonderful will happen.

1. Thank you, Lord, for my new life in Christ.

The Apostle Paul wrote that the person who has joined with Christ is a brand-new creation (2 Cor. 5:17). At first it may be hard to believe. You'll see the same old face. You'll feel the same old pain. But whatever you see, whatever you feel, you are in fact a new creation through your faith in Christ. Believe it.

Don't be afraid to put your feet on the floor, Charlie Brown, and stake out a claim on life. You are worth taking a trip to see! You are special.

St. Augustine said, "Men go abroad to wonder at the height of the mountains, at the huge waves of the sea, at the long courses of the rivers, at the vast compass of the ocean, at the circular motion of the stars; and they pass by themselves without wondering."

Why not take a trip into yourself and then send a postcard back to yourself that says, "Wish you were here to see what I see. It's beautiful. Christ is alive and working in me. I am a new creation even when I feel like the same old person. I am new because he has promised and I will not doubt it!"

2. Thank you, Lord, that the past can no longer harm me.

Imagine it. Whatever you have done in the past he has forgiven. The slate is clean. You are pardoned. You have walked from that prison a free person and you can begin anew.

Remember the pitiful character of Jacob Marley in Charles Dickens' story "A Christmas Carol?"

Ebenezer Scrooge, the flinty old miser, had retired to his chilly bedchamber to sleep. In sleep he thought to shut out the happy sound of Christmas that had irritated him all day long. He was awakened by the moaning voice and the sound of clanking chains.

"Who are you?" asked Scrooge.

"I am Marley—your old partner, Jacob Marley."

"But—but—you are chained, Marley."

"Ah, yes, I am chained. I wear the chains I forged in life. I made them link by link and of my own free will I wore them."

Our own free will, yes that is the clue—of our own free will we wear the chains of the past. Even God will not break their negative hold on us if we do not want him to. On the other hand, we would not be able to break them by ourselves. Only God can take away the past, only he can cancel the sins of yesterday.

One of the most influential persons in my life has been Chester Edwards. I credit him with my being interested in working with words and ideas. Chester is now retired but he still maintains his zest for life and his boyish enthusiasm. I have marveled at it many times. Recently he handed me a little white card with a message typed on it:

WHATEVER OUR PAST
WE ALL HAVE A SPOTLESS FUTURE.

If we give our past to God, we can have a spotless past as well, There are no tombstones in the cemetery where God buries our sins, no markers to remind us.

When our friends tell us that it is too late to change, there is a solution: change our friends.

I once heard a handsome young man say, "I have always been and I guess I will always be a victim of circumstances." His words were like a hammer of a blacksmith forging a chain to bind him to his past. Whatever his past had been, it became a long, long chain to keep him from becoming what he would like to be. Of course, the chain is not made of iron; it is made of ideas. They are more binding

We are all tempted to think we will always be what we have been. Maybe we think we will be worse than we have been. Whatever our past is, in Christ it is gone forever. Don't keep it alive, trust him!

3. Thank you, Lord, that the future holds no fear.

There are so many things we could fear: nuclear war, economic collapse, crime in the streets, cancer and heart disease, the death of a friend, a crippling accident. Let's face it: these are real and awful and common prospects for our future. But listen to Jesus' words, "Lo, I am with you always, to the close of the age" (Matt. 28:20). He has

71

overcome the world for us. He has conquered death and destroyed its fearful grip on humankind. With him we can face the future knowing all is well.

4. Thank you, Lord, for this new day and all it holds for me both good and bad.

Who can guess what circumstances will surround us during the next twenty-four hours? The word *circumstances* comes from two Latin words meaning "around" and "stand." Circumstances, then, are the things that stand around us, whether they are good or bad. It is easy to celebrate the good that comes our way and difficult to celebrate the bad. Charlie knows well just how difficult it is.

You are in good company while you are losing. Let me quote something from Emerson: "Our strength grows out of our weakness. The imagination which arms itself with secret forces does not awaken until we are pricked and stung and sorely assailed."

The Apostle Paul discovered this earlier. He wrote, "When I am weak, then I am strong" (2 Cor. 12:10). For him, God's strength was made perfect in weakness.

Don't lament your mistakes. They may be the best things that ever happened to you. After all, they tell some very nice things about you. If you hadn't tried to do something you wouldn't have failed. Be glad you tried. Failures are powerful teachers. We must, of course, be willing to learn from them. Concentrate on what you learned from them.

When you are tempted to criticize your judgment, congratulate yourself on your daring. Fear of failure keeps you postponing your education. At the end of the day as at the beginning, thank God for your failures. Thank him for his presence and for the good that came into your life today. And tomorrow begin anew.

5. *Lord, I give this day to you. Work in me and work through me as you will.*

This is the one magic key to "living like a king's kid": you are not the king, God is.

Feeling good about yourself depends upon recognizing this relationship. Otherwise, you are like the dethroned sovereign who is exiled on a hostile shore. He wanders about the earth trying to convince anyone who will listen, "I am in charge around here." But even with a royal crest on his knapsack, he does not command much respect.

When we bow to God's authority we become royalty ourselves.

When the kingdom of God is within us, we are not fearful of the world around us. "Greater is he that is in you than he that is in the world," Jesus said.

Don't give in to all those doubts. In this new relationship, you are unconquerable because your King is.

It shouldn't surprise you that along with the ruler will come some rules. After all, the kingdom within you is not a democracy or even a republic. It is an absolute monarchy. Your personal power comes to an end, but don't let that frighten you. This is not what it sounds like at first.

Everything has two ends—a beginning and a final end. To

be subject to God's power means that you are able to use that power. When you are not subject to God's power, you are limited to your own power. When you are not subject to God's wisdom you have only your own. How quickly our own power and wisdom are exhausted! How impossible it is to exhaust God's resources!

God does not make us slaves or servants; he makes us his children. Being the children of a king makes us royalty. We must live and act like children of the King.

Wonderfully, this kind of self-image does not depend on accomplishments but relationships. We can feel good about ourselves not primarily because of who we are but whose we are. There is a difference.

The wind-me-up-so-I-can-tell-you-how-great-I-am school of psychology comes off a very poor second to the concept of the kingdom of God. We are confident not because of what we have become but because of where we have come from.

You and I know, Charlie Brown, that Snoopy charms the whole world. He has that charm that comes naturally to animals. They don't have to explain their ancestry; they simply accept it.

When we accept the family relationship in the kingdom of God, we don't need to apologize. We are truly special.

While it is true that we all look forward to the final moments in history when the "kingdoms of this world become the kingdoms of our God and of Christ," we are not orphans until that time. The Kingdom is now.

Perhaps we speculate about the great battle with the kingdoms of the world because we do not want to think about the battle for the throne in our own hearts.

Dr. Kenneth Scott Foreman, beloved teacher at Louisville Presbyterian Seminary, often shared this poem with us:

> I'm really not one person
> But within me is a crowd.
> There's one of me that's humble
> And one of me that's proud.
> There's one who cares nothing
> For fame and worldly self.
> The other "me" is haughty,
> Thinks of no one but myself.
> There's one of me repentant
> For all my many sins.
> The other me's hardhearted
> And simply sits and grins.
> From much corroding care,
> I could at last be free.

If I could just discover
Which one of "us" is "me."

Charles Schulz is often asked, "Which one of your characters is really you?"

"Probably there's a little of me in all of them," he says.

"How can I fight the world," lamented a college girl, "when I have a civil war inside me?"

Answer: Pick up the guidebook and move into the Kingdom. Or more accurately, let the Kingdom move into you.

It has become popular to think that internal conflict is normal. Average it may be. Normal? No. It is not what God intended.

Fortunately, the paradox of power is that when we surrender to God's power, we become victorious. When we say one gigantic yes to God's will, we are able to say no to the manipulative schemes of selfish people.

76

The answer to Dr. Foreman's poem—which, may I add, was certainly not his problem—is really simple. If there are many separate selves within us, we have only to lead them to the throne at the center of our world. We submit them all to Jesus.

Each day, as we pray these prayers, we surrender a little bit more of our life to his control. And as a result, as his Spirit gains control in our lives, we watch in growing joyful surprise how our thoughts and words and deeds are becoming more and more like his.

Even our brothers and sisters in Christ may be difficult to deal with.

Chapter 7
My Old Friends and
My New Friends

It is difficult enough to handle our doubts and our own fears the morning after we decide that the Doctor is in. But to make matters worse we have to go out and face our friends with the news of our decision. Sharing our new dreams with old friends can be very, very frustrating.

After that first quizzical look, that first raised eyebrow, that first suppressed smile, it is easy to decide to give up friends forever. Who needs them? we ask ourselves. Better to make it alone. Even our brothers and sisters in Christ may be difficult to deal with. New friends or old can be quite the burden. So the temptation comes to get rid of our friends altogether. Admit it. It looks like common sense. We think, If only I could get away from people for a while I could find myself.

Who has not had the feeling? Who has not spoken it to herself or himself? If it were possible to take the schedule of any day and fashion it as children take clay in their hands, and if it were possible to solve all the problems in terms of one's self, wouldn't life be smoother? For a while at least?

But somehow life is not the same without friendship. We seem to be half of something else—or maybe someone else. It's difficult to clap with just one hand. It takes two.

John Donne said it: "No man is an island entire unto himself."

We need friends. We need our old friends who may not yet believe the Doctor is in. In earlier years pastors and priests, Sunday school teachers and Christian parents have encouraged new believers to drop their old nonbelieving friends and spend all their time with new friends in Christ's body. And certainly some old friends whose effect on our lives has been destructive, even evil, should be abandoned. But old friends from the past whose influence has been positive and loving should not be abandoned regardless of where they might be in their own spiritual pilgrimages.

We need new friends in the church as well. Sometimes church groups can be unknowingly cliquish and hard to break into. You remember how it felt to move into a new school or job or neighborhood. It's hard to begin building new friendships anywhere. *But we need to begin.* To build friendships with our Christian brothers and sisters can mean the difference in our own growth and development in the faith. But there are a few warning signs along the way:

1. Beware those friends who don't like to see you change because they want you to stay exactly as you are.

That sounds wonderful! My friends don't want to change me; they like me just as I am. They accept me just as I am with all my faults and weaknesses.

Of course they accept you and, since you want to be accepted, you don't change. You keep on being just what you have always been, and you know God doesn't like that. God loves you just as you are, but he loves you too much to let you stay that way.

So in a sense, God is our enemy, our assailant. No wonder we try to run away from him even though we know we should not.

2. Beware those friends who don't want us to change because they like themselves just as they are.

When we start dreaming of being a better person and, what is worse, when we actually start to become that better person, some friends may do their best to "bring us back to our senses." Why? Simply because the changes they can see in us bring judgment on them.

If you have tried to go on a diet, who will try to talk you out of it? Your fat friends, of course. And if you manage to lose twenty pounds in spite of their advice, how will they react? Will they praise you for your courage and discipline? Hardly. Instead they will say, "You don't look well; your face seems haggard. I really liked you better when you were plump."

If you dare to share your serious dreams with them, they do their best to get you to forget them.

3. Beware those friends who always comfort you when you really need to be confronted.

If we occasionally feel guilty about something we have done or about something we should have done and didn't, how do your friends react? If they gather around you and say, "Don't feel bad; we like you. We understand you. Don't get upset. Relax. This feeling of guilt will pass away," beware.

We may too easily submit to their kindness. Who doesn't like to be comforted! Turn up the music and let's forget this sick obsession with sin. Forget it? How?

The only way to deal with sin is to admit it. Naturally there are friends who don't want this to happen. First they feel righteous because they are comforting us, pouring love and acceptance on us like healing oil. Second, they don't want to face sin in their own lives. Accepting others drowns out their need for repentance.

The loving laughter of those friends may drown out the voice from above us and from within us, the voice that could bring us forgiveness and renewal. The comfort of friends can be the kiss of death.

It is the normal function of sinners to tell other sinners that they are normal, to tell miserable people that they are really happy, and to tell fantasizing people that they are really facing reality. It is normal for sinners to comfort one another with lies. The devil is the father of lies.

The devil lies not only about our condition but about the possibility of our changing it. It is the devil who tunes our hearts to listen to the clamor without instead of the claims within. The devil makes us ashamed of our divine origin and proud of our shameful orgies.

Certainly the devil never appears as a red-suited, leering enemy. He does not carry a three-pronged fork to frighten us. On the contrary, he speaks with the oily-smooth voice of acceptance. He masquerades as a friend telling us that any twinge of guilt or any godly sorrow is psychopathic. He surrounds us with a fawning friend who picks us up when we occasionally stumble across some abrasive truth, bandages our wounded vanity, and tells us that we will get over it.

Sin not only lets us miss the mark of God's high calling but insists on drawing a bull's-eye around the place where our chance arrow has hit so that we have the illusion of not missing anything.

If the Doctor within us attempts spiritual surgery, beware the friends who hasten to rouge our cheeks and plump our pillow and tell us that we are looking good.

Like Lucy, the devil mocks our sincere quest to find the will of God and says, "Sure, I understand perfectly—but forget it."

4. Beware those friends who want us to live up to their expectations and not necessarily God's expectations.

It is natural for friends to want us to fit into their plans. What about God's plans?

Remember the time your friends dug away at your pitcher's mound, Charlie Brown? As you walked out to the ball park, you thought of yourself as a fireball pitcher. You strode to the mound confidently. You were undermined by your friends.

85

A few more friends and you would be completely undermined.

It's not that these friends want to manipulate us. They simply want us to fit into their plans. We want to fit into the kingdom of God. They want us to blend with the neighborhood. God wants us to live like royalty. Our friends want us to move in with the common people.

The mountain of our vision may be whittled down by friends who have no yen for the heights; they simply want some dirt for their flower pots. And we are sacrificed to their plans.

5. *Beware those friends who want you to conform to them.*

Peer pressure is a powerful force. It is not that we willingly abandon our dreams; we are simply embarrassed by them.

"Youth gathers materials to build of his life a palace, but at the age thirty concludes to build a woodshed," said Henry David Thoreau.

Why? Why do we miss the mark? Why sin?

Often our dreams are trampled under the feet of disillusioned friends. Dreams lie in ashes around their feet, and to listen to yours merely stirs the painful memories of the days when they were not afraid to hope.

Everyone dreams at some time in their lives. Hang on to your dreams, Charlie Brown. If you have to choose between your dreams and your friends, hang on to your dreams. Then again perhaps your friends need a friend who will take the risk and tell them the truth. Stand up for your dreams, Charlie, and watch your friends catch the spirit.

86

Let's quit all this negative talk about friendship—all these warnings—and get on with the positive side. Don't become afraid of your friends. Stand up to them. Tell them when they're getting in the way. They'll change. They'll come around. Be glad! You're going to need them.

Praise a friend who makes you happy.

Charlie, it must be something to have a friend like Lucy. At least she keeps you posted on her needs and how you can meet them. Too many friends just wait idly by. They have needs that you could meet to make them happier, to help them get through the long dark night, and to help them survive, but most of the time you're going to have to guess what those needs are and how you can meet them.

When visiting an ancient mountain cloister a young nun found that just before she asked for something it would be automatically provided. If she wanted butter for her bread, it was passed to her before she asked. If she had a question, someone volunteered an answer before she asked it. Finally she asked the mother superior, "How do the sisters know I have need before I even ask?" The old woman answered, "My dear, it is the way of Christ—to watch for need and meet it before you're even asked."

Praise a friend who brings you new ideas.

Christopher Morley once wrote,

"No man has enough bees in his own bonnet
To pollinate the flowers of his own mind.
Import me a few strange notions.

Friends who confront us are more valuable than friends who don't. Friends who make us think, feel, laugh, cry, and argue are better than friends who don't. Reward your friend who is alive to new ideas and is not afraid to risk your friendship by dragging you kicking and screaming into some new thought.

Don't be afraid of nonbelievers who test you. The truth is that Christ can survive quite an intellectual battering. If he stumps you, admit it. Then determine to find the answers

87

and bring up the discussion again when you have more information. If friends laugh at an idea, don't get defensive and storm away. Ask them why they're laughing and in that quiet moment you may uncover all kinds of exciting issues just below the nervous laughter. Let friends confront, convict, and try to convince you and in the process you will grow.

Praise a friend who stays with you in times of trouble.

Peppermint Patty may be taking friendship one step too far when she offers to "shorten his life span," but how precious the friend who doesn't flee the scene when we are about to lose the battle. Perhaps the saddest example is the problem of maintaining friendship when one is dying. A terminal cancer patient once told me, "As soon as my friends learned that I was dying, they disappeared. They didn't know how to help me. They felt terrible to see me losing weight. They felt awkward trying to keep up a conversation in my hospital room and one by one they've gone."

It is difficult to be with a friend who is under tremendous pressure. It is painful to walk with a friend through the traumas of life or death, but those are the times our friends need us the most. They don't expect answers. They know we don't have easy solutions. They only need us by their side to laugh with them when life or death seems silly and to cry with them when emotional or physical pain grows beyond the bearing. Praise your friend who stays with you in times of trouble. That friend is, as Solomon writes, worth more than gold.

Praise a friend who helps you keep your commitments.

Charlie, when Lucy hears your dreams, even the simple ones, and in a word destroys them, she is not your friend. Even if friends don't agree with our dreams, our priorities, and our commitments, they are responsible to help us see them realized. That doesn't mean they must simply go along with our values when they conflict with their own. A good friend will help us test and try our commitments to see if they are worthy. But once a commitment is established, our friends are only friends when they help us keep them.

For example, take our commitment to Christ and his kingdom. Friends inside or outside belief who interfere with that commitment, who get in the way of our spiritual growth, who tease and downgrade and satirize, are destructive. But friends who value our commitment to Christ, even if they don't agree, work to see that dream come true.

Our commitment to a husband or wife, or to another friend should also be valued by our friends. People who get in the way of long-established relationships are dangerous. But friends who value our commitments to other people and help us maintain them are of great worth.

Our real friends will try to discover who we are and to what and to whom we are committed and then will use their friendship to help us be true to those commitments and to ourselves. Praise that kind of friend.

Praise your friend for just being friendly.

Solomon the Wise wrote three thousand years ago, "To have friends, you must show yourself friendly." How often we simply assume that our friends are rewarded by our friendship. How seldom we take time to tell them in little ways or in big, expensive ones how grateful we are for their friendship and how important their friendship is to us.

Pick up the phone today and call a friend just to say thanks. Today send an unexpected card or letter or singing telegram to a friend just to express appreciation. Invite a friend to lunch (and then pay the tab). Every dime you invest in appreciating a friend who loves you, who confronts you, who stands with you in times of trouble, who helps you see your kingdom dream come true, is money well spent.

It is easy to look back. Kingdom folk often make that mistake. They spend an entire lifetime replaying the moment when they entered the kingdom of heaven.

Chapter 8
My New Mind

As a brand-new member of God's kingdom family you have to decide immediately where you are going to live. Oh, your house address can stay the same, but where will your mind reside?

There are brothers and sisters who live too much in the past.

It is easy, Charlie Brown, to look back. It is a good feeling to remember those happy days now gone and all the joy they brought you.

Kingdom folk often make the same mistake. They live in the past. They spend an entire spiritual lifetime replaying that wonderful moment when they entered the Kingdom and began their life of faith. They celebrate their new birthday over and over again.

Or they make a more subtle mistake. Christ's life, death, and resurrection actually happened two thousand years ago in a Roman colony on the eastern shores of the Mediterranean. What Jesus said and did back then is still at the heart of Kingdom life. Our new life in Christ began then but it did not end then. To spend our spiritual lives remembering God's Son only as a bearded Jew preaching in a Palestinian desert or as a bleeding servant on a rugged cross or as the newly risen Lord standing outside an empty tomb is not enough. Through his Holy Spirit, Jesus is as alive and active now in our lives as he was alive and active in the lives of Peter, James, and John. That's what his Spirit is about. The Kingdom is not yesterday; the Kingdom is now.

The only words Jesus used about his kingdom were *now* words. He was constantly using the verb *is.* To be sure, when we think about God, we always have to understand that he *is,* not *was.*

The problem is not a grammatical one; it's theological. If we relegate all of God's activity to the past, then we may just as well put him in a wax museum and label him "ancient history."

Whatever God did for the people of the past he did while he was their contemporary. It was a *now* experience for them.

Life has to be a *now* experience for us as well.

There are brothers and sisters who live too much in the future.

It isn't wrong to look to the stars, to wonder about the future. In fact, President Theodore Roosevelt stargazed to remind him of his own humility. But too many of our brothers and sisters have taken up stargazing as a full-time vocation.

Millions of people are trying to guess what will happen to planet Earth. Will Christ come again and what will he do when he comes?

There is a danger in too much speculation about the coming King. We may forget that the King has already come once and he has set up a kingdom that is here now.

Why are we so obsessed with our speculations about when Christ will return? What is the strange fascination? Read Jesus' words in the New Testament. He spent very little time talking about the future. In fact, he said plainly, "Watch therefore, for ye know neither the day nor the hour wherein the Son of man cometh" (Matt. 25:13). What Jesus talked about and made perfectly clear is what he expects from us now!

Still, newspapers frequently carry stories of people who go to remote hillsides to wait the coming of Christ. Others sell their possessions and adorn themselves in white robes to be ready. Books and bumper stickers talk of the Second Coming.

Is it fair to ask if much of this thought about the coming kingdom is an escape for us? If we aren't careful we will simply sit and wait until the end of time and then admit that we were a part of the eternal kingdom of God and missed our chance to experience it. Christ will return. That much is clear! The rest of those questions—When will he return? How will he be known?—are all speculation. Don't spend too much time on them.

Join our brothers and sisters who live in the present.
Look for them! They are everywhere—men and women who believe the kingdom of God is *now*. Their past is forgiven. Their future is secure. They are about God's kingdom now. They are working with God to transform the present. In his name they are bringing new life to a dying world.

97

Once we are convinced that God operates in the present we avoid a nostalgic look back and fruitless speculation about the future.

In the parables about the kingdom of God in the New Testament we are warned that whenever the king returned, he wanted to find his servants busily working—not merely looking down the road.

Live now! There are at least three underlying biblical truths that will help you get started.

1. Believe the kingdom of God is in you now.

Remember the words of Jesus? "The kingdom of God is within you" (Luke 17:21). These words came when the shouting troops of Caesar were a constant reminder that Palestine was an occupied country. No Jew could walk down the street without being reminded of overpowering forces all around.

The wistful hope of every Jew was that some Messiah would come on a white horse and mobilize an army. With this army he would cast the enemy into the sea. They would wait for such a Messiah even though they might wait endlessly. They saw the kingdom of God in terms of armies and soldiers and generals, a kingdom outside them, a leader ordering them about. When Jesus didn't go along with their ideas, it was only natural that the crowds would pressure him to declare his intention. Just what did he have in mind?

He decided to let them wait no longer. He said, "The Kingdom of God cometh not with observation: Neither shall they say, Lo here! or, lo there! for, behold, the kingdom of God is within you" (Luke 17:20-21). That was a mind-boggling idea. It still is.

Our enemies today are not the same ones who brought fear to the people of Jesus' day, but we do have enemies. We are opposed by those who would keep us from believing that the kingdom of God is real because we cannot see it. There are those who would keep us from believing God himself is working within us now because we may not feel him. Perhaps, in fact, our very worst enemy is our own doubt. So we need to start by reshaping our own mind. Say it to yourself. Never stop believing it. "I believe the kingdom of God is working in me now!"

"Each of us is obliged to be his own center," said Dean Inge, "but he is not obliged to be his own circumference." The "I" is a good place to start; it's just a poor place to stop.

A fascinating secular insight comes from Buckminster Fuller, the inventive genius and student of the world:

"The universe is a locked safe with the combination on the inside."

Day after day in the heart of primitive Africa, Dr. Albert Schweitzer battled both disease and the ignorance that brought it. After years of work and thought he wrote in his diary: "Each patient carries his own doctor with him. They come to us not knowing that truth. We are at our best when we give the doctor that resides within a chance to work."

If we were to go from our highly civilized cities to look at Schweitzer's primitive hospital, we would scarcely recognize it as a hospital. The crude buildings would look more like chicken coops than clinics. We would wonder how it could be possible to practice medicine in a place like this. Surely, we would think, brick buildings and gleaming chrome instruments would be more effective.

Schweitzer knew that healing takes place the same way in both kinds of places. It has to come from within. Dr. Schweitzer's statement was written only after his years of work and thought had proved it. The kingdom within us is more important than the world around us—whether that world is the steamy equatorial jungle or the jet-paced world of science.

Whether there is agreement from the White House, Number 10 Downing Street, the Vatican, or the wild kingdom of animals, the principle is the same. The kingdom within rules.

If we don't believe the kingdom of God is within, if we are at war within ourselves, no other battles are needed. We are defeated.

How do we think we will bring peace to the world when there is no peace in us? We are constantly pressured to think about all the problems around us, yet to think about ourselves seems almost non-Christian and selfish. Settle it now once and for all. The kingdom of God is within me now. God is inside me now.

2. *Believe that God within is reshaping you into something beautiful.*

For each of us it is difficult to believe that we are more than average. It seems impossible in light of the billions of people on the globe that we are special to anyone, let alone special to God. But it is true. The kingdom of God is within us. God is at work in our minds changing us into that dream he has for us. So quit rejecting yourself. God doesn't.

It is common knowledge among students of human nature that people who reject themselves are often rejected by others. Tragically, the more love they need from others the less of it they get.

The great news is that God has great plans for you. If you will let him rule your life, you will have a chance to discover what those plans are. It seems that God reveals his secrets one at a time. If we do not explore through obedience the voice of God today, we will not know what he had planned for tomorrow.

Whatever he wants to do, however, will have to be done through us. As Fuller says, the combination to the locked world is on the inside—inside us.

You are special. There is no one else like you. Everything about you is a miracle of intricate design—and it was designed for something! What?

Each time scientists explore the physical or the mental world of human beings they uncover new and exciting frontiers for further exploration. To think that all of this just happened by some kind of cosmic accident is as absurd as to imagine the astronauts' exploring the moon, finding a ticking watch with the right time, and remarking casually, "Things like this simply happen if you leave them alone long enough.

William Wordsworth looked at the possibility of our living beyond this world by imagining how we came into it:

100

Our birth is but a sleep and a forgetting;
The soul that rises with us,
Our life's star
Has somewhere else its setting
And cometh from afar.
Not in utter nakedness nor forgetfulness
But trailing clouds of glory do we come
From heaven that is our home.

Imagine it! In biblical terms we are created "in the image of God" (Gen. 1:27). In modern words, God made you to be like himself. He has a wonderful dream for your life and he is within you working to see that dream come true.

3. Believe that you can help God do his work in you.
Learn to think Kingdom thoughts. Our thoughts have been programmed from our infancy. We have been told in whispers and in screams who everyone else thinks we are. We are father, mother, son, or daughter. We are rich or poor. We are black or white, red or yellow. We are too tall or too short, too fat or too skinny. It's taken a lifetime to program us but now we believe it.

Paul said, "In Christ . . . all things are become new" (2 Cor. 5:17). He also said with the Kingdom in us we are neither "Jew nor Greek . . . male nor female" (Gal. 3:28). All those limiting, narrow, crippling thoughts about ourselves have to go. God's voice inside whispering his dream for us must drown out all those other voices.

Listen to a true story.

A strange fire burned in the young man's eyes as he picked up the heavy dictionary. The dictionary itself was a part of the amazing change that was taking place in his mind. He had been told that words were powerful, so he bought a dictionary so that he could use some of that power—the power of words.

In a few moments he found the word he wanted. Then with a pair of scissors he clipped it from the dictionary. Crumpling it in his hand, he threw it into the fire.

"There, I have done it," he said. "I have taken the word *impossible* out of my life forever."

I applaud him. As deeply as I love books, I love people more. If a book must be mutilated so that a person may be free from captivity to words, I say attack the books.

The truth is plain. If we are going to change our lives—or if we are going to be changed by a new power within us—we will have to learn a new way of thinking. We will have to learn to think like God's people, the citizens of the new kingdom, members of his family.

"If ye have faith as a grain of mustard seed . . . nothing shall be impossible unto you," said Jesus (Matt. 17:20).

While it is easy to read these words, it is difficult for us to look inside our minds and discover all the little walls and compartments that limit the flow of this marvelous promise. Only occasionally does it spill over our mental restrictions and bring us a miracle. Merely thinking the word *impossible* builds walls within us—walls that keep God out.

Learn to speak Kingdom language. Now that you have moved into the Kingdom of God—or more correctly the kingdom of God has moved within you—you must learn to speak the language. It is a language of faith, optimism, and blessing. To speak optimistically or happily in the middle of a world of pagan pessimism may sound as strange to the people around you as Chinese would sound to the residents of Birmingham, Alabama. But it is the language you must learn, the language you must speak.

Learning to talk like a citizen of the kingdom of God is important. After all, if we are going to live in this kingdom we need to know how to communicate.

Try to imagine life in the United States without any knowledge of the English language. To buy a tube of toothpaste would be a major accomplishment. To ask directions would require an interpreter. The simplest act of our everyday life would be frustrating beyond description. And, horrible thought, if we didn't know the language we couldn't even describe our frustration.

Maybe the trouble is language itself. We all know what we mean, but we live in a world in which nobody else understands.

You will hear Kingdom talkers with tongues of gold, but don't worry. You may not play Beethoven yet, but start trying. A simple prayer, a word of praise, a one-verse chorus, and one day you'll speak the language, too. Try!

If we *cannot* talk we must remain silent. Silence may be golden, but it is sometimes a gilded death.

I have read that when Frederick II was emperor of Sicily in the thirteenth century he tried an ambitious experiment. As he thought about the world and of his own country, it seemed to him that the principal business of most nations was making war. Why? he asked himself.

It must be that people do not understand one another, he

thought. But why don't they understand one another? Obviously they speak different languages.

Then Frederick reasoned that if all people spoke the same language they might be able to communicate, and perhaps with communication would come understanding. Could it be possible, he asked himself, that people might naturally speak the *same* language—a universal language—if they were not taught the language of their parents?

He decided to conduct an experiment. He arranged to separate a group of newborn infants from their natural parents and place them under the care of foster parents. These foster parents would care for the babies in every way, but they were not to speak to them. The babies were not to hear the sound of human speech. In this way, thought Frederick, we will find out if there is some form of speech that comes without being taught. He imagined that this might be Hebrew.

What happened?

Of course, the babies did not learn to talk. More tragic, however, the babies died.

Our lives depend upon our ability to communicate. This is true in our physical existence, but it is even more true of our citizenship in the kingdom of heaven.

If you had never seen a football game and were suddenly transplanted into the bleachers of an exciting game, you would be as mystified as if you were put down in the middle of pure chaos. What would it mean to you to see men running up and down a field, falling down on the ground and then being covered with human bodies? You would notice that the action centered around carrying a ball back and forth on the field for several hours. Even more confusing would be the commentator's announcement that after the ball had been rubbed in the earth for fifteen minutes someone had a first down.

The Bible is at the heart of Kingdom thought and language. Read it. Get a translation that you can both enjoy and understand. Don't give up if you don't understand everything. Keep reading.

Often the songs sung in churches sound like a foreign language to people who have not heard them before. But hymns and gospel choruses, too, are part of Kingdom language. Don't abandon these old songs. Learn and teach the language of Zion—the vocabulary of the Kingdom. It doesn't mean we must speak in King James English. Kingdom talk can be ancient or modern. It can be in English, Japanese, or Croatian, in sign language or song. Whatever you speak, learn to speak the language of God's people. We must learn to use our voices creatively in his name or we will use them destructively. We will use either words that become friends or words that destroy us.

One of the most amazing verses in the Bible is in the book of wisdom—Proverbs. "Death and life are in the power of the tongue: and they that love it shall eat the fruit thereof" (18:21). What you talk about you will become. "That every idle word that men shall speak, they shall give account," said Jesus. "For by thy words thou shalt be justified, and by thy words thou shalt be condemned" (Matt. 12:36-37).

Every word we speak has the power to bless us or curse us. We can either liberate or imprison ourselves by our language. In a sense, every word is a self-fulfilling prophecy. Words are blueprints of our future. To talk is to write our diary in advance.

To talk constantly about negative, discouraging things is to set in motion not only the mood of discouragement but the bleak facts it envisions. To allow the despair of our age to color our conversation as Christians is to show the world that we have not truly understood the kingdom within.

To talk nonstop about our troubles is like fertilizing weeds. We should not be surprised at the harvest from the seed-words our lips have planted.

To make the transition from the critical to the constructive may be difficult, but it is not impossible. Nothing is.

In all of literature there is no more powerful description of this fact than the one the Apostle James gives us in the New Testament:

If anyone is never at fault in what he says, he is a perfect man, able to keep his whole body in check.
When we put bits into the mouths of horses to make them obey us, we can turn the whole animal. Or take ships as an example. Although they are so large and are driven of strong winds, they are steered by a very small rudder wherever the pilot wants to go. Likewise the tongue is a small part of the body, but it makes great boasts. Consider what a great forest is set on fire by a small spark. The tongue also is a fire, a world of evil

among the parts of the body. It corrupts the whole
person, sets the whole course of his life on fire, and is
itself set on fire by hell.

—James 3:2-6, NIV

Talk is far from cheap. It may be the most expensive thing
in the world. Your words give life or death. Learn the
vocabulary of the Kingdom. Speak God's words and give
life.

A song by Barney Warren deserves to be played by a
military band. It is a strong and courageous statement about
the kingdom of God. It is an example of both the thoughts
and the words of the Kingdom. While it is almost sacrilege
to give these words with nothing but the click-clack of my
typewriter as accompaniment, this is how it will reach you.

There's a theme that is sweet to my mem'ry.
There's a joy that I cannot express,
There's a treasure that gladdens my being,
'Tis the kingdom of God's righteousness.

Tis a kingdom of peace, it is reigning within.
It shall ever increase in my soul;
We possess it right here
When he saves from all sin
And 'twill last while the ages shall roll.

There's a scene of its grandness before me,
Of its greatness there can be no end.
It is joy, it is peace, it is glory,
In my heart, how these riches do blend!

I am lost in its splendor and beauty,
To its ne'er fading heights I would rise,
Till I see the King come to receive me,
And explore it with him in the skies.

What a pleasure in life it is bringing!
What assurance and hope ever bright!

107

O what rapture and bliss are awaiting,
When our faith shall be lost in the sight!

"Let me write the songs of a people," said a philosopher, "and I care not who writes their books." If this song could become the theme for Christians, it might change their world. It is a good marching song for citizens of the heavenly kingdom. It is elementary Kingdom talk. Try it.

We all worry. We may paste clever quotations about the futility of worry on our refrigerators, but still we worry.

Chapter 9
My New Body

As the God within goes to work on "kingdomizing" our minds (thoughts, words, and deeds), he also goes to work on our bodies. So Charlie, you know how it feels to have a "cheap stomach." But for some of the kingdom folk reading this letter to you, suffering may go far beyond a tummyache.

Some of you may have terminal cancer. Others suffer from heart disease or emphysema or multiple sclerosis. You may be crippled from birth or have recently been crippled in a tragic accident or by an unexpected disease. Now you have entered the Kingdom. Now God lives and works within you. You have the right to ask, What about my physical (or emotional) suffering? Will God heal me?

My wife, Berny, is from the mountains of southwest Virginia. She has a manner of speaking that makes at least two syllables out of most one-syllable words. Do not let that mislead you. She talks slowly but she thinks fast.

One day I noticed that she didn't seem to be her usual vivacious self, so I said, "Honey, are you sick?"

"I sure hope I'm sick, because I would hate to feel like this if I'm well," she responded.

Does that sound as though I have a complaining neurotic on my hands? Certainly not. I have an intelligent, sensitive wife. Her answer made me feel good and it amused me. It gave me a tremendous hope for her recovery.

She did not like feeling pain or discomfort. She knew that illness is not the way God planned it. So how should she respond—how should we all respond—to any physical or emotional malady that cripples us, inhibits our growth, and threatens to keep us from becoming what God dreams us to be?

1. We can worry.

Of course, we remind ourselves that worry is a poorly paid vocation, but still we worry. We may even paste clever quotations about the futility of worry on our refrigerators, but still we worry. Someone once wrote,

112

The worst of my foes,
Are my worries and woes,
And troubles that never come true.

Still we worry. We know that worry is building bridges over rivers we may never have to cross, but we worry. We know that worry is the interest we pay when we borrow trouble. Still we worry.

It becomes more complicated as we worry about our inability to stop worrying.

Worry is a normal response to emotional or physical crises, but worry only makes it worse. When our anxieties have anxieties we are on a downward spiral that could destroy us. Still, knowing that worry is evil does not help us stop worrying, let alone get well.

2. We can criticize ourselves.

Somehow it seems almost redemptive to hate ourselves for what we've done to bring on our physical or emotional problems. We can live on regret and self-hatred. We can see ourselves as failures because we didn't live up to our potential and we contributed to the suffering. We know that God promises us a much better life than we manage to live; we need to know also that God is long-suffering and patient. He does not expel us from class because we are slow learners in the school of grace.

Self-hatred is a denial not only of ourselves but of God. To be too critical of ourselves is to forget what God our creator has done for us in Christ and what he can do to our bodies and our minds.

The Book of James in the New Testament talks wryly of this kind of spiritual split personality that makes mental or physical health impossible.

But the tongue can no man tame; it is an unruly evil full of deadly poison. Therewith bless we God, even the

113

Father, and therewith curse we men, which are made in the similitude of God. Out of the mouth proceedeth blessing and cursing . . . These things ought not so to be.

—James 3:8-10

If we despise ourselves—even our faltering and failing selves—we reflect on the wisdom and will of the Creator. If God does not despise us to talk lowly of us—not even in sickness or failure—should we criticize ourselves?

3. We can deny our sickness or pain.

It doesn't help but we do it. I heard a radio commentator report that in 1981 more Valium was sold to women in America than all other pills combined. Valium is a depressant that keeps people from feeling pain or anxiety. Could it be possible that people use billions of pills and millions of dollars to help them escape their physical and emotional pain?

There are other ways of escaping temporarily. They do not work either, but among the list are drugs, alcohol, synthetic faith that denies pain, and a thousand worthless cures that give us false hope. All of these seem to help temporarily, but when their effects are gone, the problem is still with us.

Dunn and Bradstreet, the financial statisticians, made a study of business failures. They concluded that 95 percent of the failures were caused by keeping inadequate records. Though the businesses were ailing and profits were declining, no one seemed to know until it was too late. The proprietors assumed that everything was going all right. Not until the businesses collapsed did they realize something was wrong.

The first step in curing the ills of a failing business is to admit that it is sick. Then perhaps a doctor can be found.

As we trace the ministry of Jesus we discover that he often diagnosed the sickness before he cured it. "What do you want me to do for you?" he asked blind Bartimaeus.

"That I might receive my sight," said the man.

While it seems highly ridiculous to ask a blind man what is wrong with him, this confession seemed important to

Jesus. Unless Bartimaeus understood that he had a sickness there was little chance that he could be healed.

He might actually have preferred the world of blackness and begging to the world of light and labor. Such things have happened.

Do you ever feel like running away either physically or psychologically? Where would you go?

The believer may say, "Well of course when we get to heaven all our problems will be over. Indeed they will. But few of us are willing to abandon this earth voluntarily now. We are in no hurry to make that dramatic escape.

"In the world you have tribulation," said Jesus. He knows that even though the kingdom of God will triumph totally, there will be many battles for believers before that final victory. Our weapons are not physical, but they are weapons, nonetheless, and not ornaments on the walls of our spiritual family rooms. The world is here—and so are we.

If we cannot escape physical or emotional illnesses, what can we do about them? How do we deal with pain? These are questions as old as humankind and as up to date as the moment your hand reaches for the aspirin.

The world abounds with advice. Here are two illustrations. One is from the perceptive pen of Charles Schulz and one is from an ancient medical journal. The first illustrates how we feel about our human ignorance and weakness when facing serious illness. The second illustrates the power of God as healer.

First Schulz:

Now from the medical journal. Let us look over the doctor's shoulder.

Three thousand years ago a young doctor squinted at the writings before him. They were the latest scientific discoveries of the most brilliant men of his time. They were indeed the result of centuries of research and experiment. But they were difficult to believe.

True, the names of the scientists were familiar to him. To Moses, they had been his teachers at the university—and the university was known throughout the world as a center of learning. These men were quoted with respect and reverence. Surely there was no way he could doubt what they had written. Was he, a young man beginning his ministry of healing, wiser than they?

Yes, he thought, I may be wiser than they. They have the advantage of education—but they also have the disadvantage of education. Education is often the simple passing of information from one generation to the next. Sometimes this information is wrong, even though it is respected.

It was a bold thought, a risky thought. The lives of those he loved might be endangered if he dared to trust his own ideas. Somehow the doctors all around him did not agree with the voice of his own mind—the Doctor within.

Would his patients die? Of course they might, but people were dying all around him, even with the historic treatments that were given by the other physicians. He bent his head to read these respected medical journals one more time.

To prevent hair from turning grey, anoint it with the blood of a black calf which has been boiled in oil, or with the fat of a rattlesnake. To save victims bitten by poisonous snakes, give them magic water to drink—water that has been poured over a special idol. To embedded splinters apply worms' blood and asses' dung.

These were the instructions of the medical journals. But they left in their wake scores of diseased and dying people. There must be a better way.

As though compelled by a strange inner power, Moses' hand began to write the words that seemed to rise from deep within him.

If thou wilt diligently hearken to the voice of the Lord thy

God, and wilt do that which is right in his sight, and wilt give ear to his commandments, and keep all his statutes, I will put none of these diseases upon thee, which I have brought upon the Egyptians: for I am the Lord that healeth thee.

—Exodus 15:26

There it is. From the earliest Old Testament writings of Moses to God's people, the Jews, God promised his people, "I am the Lord who heals you." And so throughout Old and New Testament literature the promise is made. God will heal our diseases.

1. *Remember, God has promised to heal us.*

Like Snoopy, we all need to face toward new horizons from time to time. For kingdom folk it is especially important at this moment in history to get new perspective on the

118

promises of God to heal our diseases. During the first century, God's healing power was evident to an astounding degree. Jesus, his disciples, and even first-century kingdom folk (described in the Book of Acts) were endowed by God with power to pray for the sick with amazing results. We are instructed in Scripture to do the same.

> Is any sick among you? Let him call for the elders of the church; and let them pray over him anointing him with oil in the name of the Lord. And the prayer of faith shall save the sick and the Lord shall raise him up, and if he has committed any sins, they shall be forgiven.
> —James 5:14-15

Among our brothers and sisters there are different responses to the promises of God's miraculous intervention in our physical and emotional health.

God still heals the sick miraculously. God is still actively healing men and women today through the prayers of his people. We believe his promises are as good now as they were in ancient times. We believe that kingdom dwellers still have the power to pray for and receive the sudden end of an illness and the instantaneous beginning of new health. Briefly, we believe that God is still very much in the miracle business. His promises can be trusted. God's promises can be trusted because his plans can be trusted.

There is a plan for your life. Discovering it means that you can begin to live as God has planned. There are rules and there is a Ruler in this world. Whatever mind it was that conceived us is wise enough to guide us.

In fact, he has left the blueprint of what he planned for us *within* us. Discovering what that plan is is the first step in becoming that person. What sort of plan is it?

R. Buckminster Fuller, mentioned in the last chapter, was one of the most creative thinkers of our generation. His fantastic mind and his daring imagination made him a welcome guest on every continent. His ideas on the conservation of energy and world ecology helped chart the plans for entire nations.

119

From Fuller's fabulous mind came plans for cities sheltered by a self-supporting dome that would make possible a year-round controlled atmosphere—an atmosphere free from pollution and bad weather.

He did not like to think about trivial things. The reason, he explained, was that when he was a small child he had a severe visual problem. He was able to see only large masses of things, never the small details. Not until he was five could he be fitted with glasses that allowed him to see normally. By that time he had already formed the habit of thinking about big things.

"On any project," Fuller said, "I always begin by thinking about the universe."

In his book *I Seem to Be a Verb,* Fuller tells of a metal that was created during the first part of our attempt to enter space. The metal is an alloy of nickel and titanium. It's technical name is Nitinol 55.

Nitinol 55 looks very much like any other alloy, but it has amazing powers. Once it has been formed into some shape, it remembers that shape forever. Even though it may be bent, twisted, or crushed, it remembers what it was made to be. Once it is heated again, it springs back instantly to its original design. But how could this be used?

Fuller suggested that a space telescope might be built of Nitinol 55. He believed, however, that such a telescope might have to be as big as a mile in diameter. Since such a bulky apparatus could not be sent into orbit, it would have to be crushed into a ball. In this way it could be hurled into the sky. When it approached the heat of the sun it would unfold. Like a flower emerging from a bud the telescope would unfold and fulfill its function in the heavens.

What a miracle that would be!

Can we believe that such a miracle could take place within us in we who are the creation of God? Is there a secret of our destiny within us? Is there the hidden memory of the plan by which we were created? No matter how much sickness and sin have distorted that original image, the memory of it is still there. The plan is intact.

The only other possibility is to believe we are nothing and become nothing. That is not scriptural. Even the comics reject the idea.

Locked within us are millions of miracles. Back of each of these is an idea—a divine idea. If Mr. Fuller can describe a human-made metal that has a memory, what would he say of the miracles and memories locked within the human mind and body?

Let us return to our discussion of Nitinol 55, the magic human-made metal that never forgets.

Have you ever watched a truckload of crushed automobiles being taken to the melting furnaces. These flattened, rusting hulks of metal are piled grotesquely on a flatbed truck. At one time each of them was a shining automobile on a showroom floor. Now, however, having outlived their usefulness, they are only scrap metal. It is almost impossible to tell that they were at one time automobiles. It is even more difficult to imagine what particular kind or model of automobile each one was. Certainly none of them is drivable.

Now let your imagination run wild. Visualize this truckload of crushed automobiles on its way to destruction. But instead of each car's being made of steel as automobiles usually are, they are made of this wonderful new metal, Nitinol 55, the metal with a memory.

As these crushed, mangled, and rusting automobiles get close to the heat of the melting furnaces, they feel a strange stirring within them. Every part feels energized. Fenders begin to snap back into shape. Engines and axles spring back to their original shape and function. Every bolt and screw is straightened. Wheels are suddenly round and perfect. The whole thing comes together and is new. Instead of a truckload of junk, we now have a dozen brand-new automobiles looking for someone with a thirty-six-coupon payment book.

While we haven't seen this kind of thing happen to crushed automobile bodies, we see this miracle every day in the kingdom of plants. This year's tulips blossom into flaming beauty. They wilt and die.

Or do they?

Certainly they wilt but they never lose the memory of their flaming beauty. It is locked within the somber brown bulb. Even though the brown bulb reveals neither the shape nor the color of its secret while it is buried in the cold winter earth, it does not forget.

Ah, spring! We have learned to look forward to it. We are not surprised when, as James Russell Lowell writes,

Every clod feels a stir of might
An instinct within it that reaches and towers
And groping blindly above it for light
Climbs to a soul in grass and flowers.

No one is surprised when tulips rise from tulip bulbs. The surprise would come if cabbages came from tulip bulbs—or if wilted, dying blossoms came from them.

We know that the flower will be like the memory locked in the seed.

The seeds of greatness are inside you, Charlie Brown. They are in all of us. Reading these words may frustrate you because today may be wintertime in your life and merely reading these words may be like looking at seed catalogs while the snow is still on the ground. Nothing good seems to be happening. Your problems and sickness are still with you. To imagine that life could be different seems like wasted dreaming.

Keep on dreaming. Don't dream of stupidity—dream of superiority. Don't dream of failing—dream of succeeding. That inner voice that talks to you during the night could very well be the voice of God.

He's not against you; he's for you. After all, if you're his child and he's the King, what does that make you?

God healed as a sign of Christ's deity. Others of us believe that Jesus healed the body of the sick and the lame to prove his power to forgive sins and heal lost souls. We believe that the followers of Jesus were given this same power after his death to prove his risen presence among us and to help establish his Church. Even now, two thousand years later, we believe God occasionally breaks the natural laws of the universe to heal someone miraculously. He does this, however, for the same reason he healed in the first century: to be a signpost to Christ and his kingdom.

God heals but through the natural processes and laws. Others of our brothers and sisters believe that the real miracle is built into our human bodies and minds. When God created us he built into our physical and mental systems processes that lead to healing. When we pray for our own or another person's healing we are allowing God to release those natural healing forces in our bodies. These natural forces are built in to protect and renew us. We believe, too, that many of our physical maladies are due to emotional stress and that physical pains are barometers that measure our use or misuse of our bodies and minds. To eliminate those pains miraculously would be to short-circuit the gift of pain that monitors our behavior and eliminate the last signals we have to warn us that we need to better manage our lives and better preserve our bodies and minds.

People assist God in our healing. Almost all of our brothers and sisters see the medical community as part of God's gift for our healing. Of course, doctors aren't perfect. Hospitals with their gleaming instruments and torturous treatments may be frightening places, but God meets us there, too, bringing through dedicated men and women of science hope and healing to his children.

The Christian community, too, can be a part of God's healing plan for us.

2. Go on praying and believing for healing.

Admit it, Charlie. Sometimes Lucy's remedies can be helpful even if she usually is the cause of your pain. People in the Kingdom, our brothers and sisters, may cause us pain, too, but in the long run they are part of our healing as well. Remember that passage from James 5:14-15? The Apostle says, "When you are sick, call the elders."

For two thousand years people have heard that command and obeyed it. Picture believers through the ages reaching out their hands to anoint the sick, showing their loving concern for one another. They've gathered in circles around the suffering in dusty desert villages and in city cathedrals to pray for the sick. They've reached out their hands to pray for the sick beside jungle streams, in prison camps, and at the scenes of disasters and catastrophes. Those hands were our hands. At the same time they were God's hands, making well our brothers and sisters through our concern. The Bible has said reach out your hands in faith believing and God

124

will heal the sick. However God answers those prayers is his business. Our task is simply to obey.

New horizons about healing will come as we search the Scripture for his word to us and follow it. Get a concordance. Look up passages relating to prayer for the sick and to healing. Study the Old and New Testament passages on healing for clues. Whatever you have or haven't seen in terms of healing miracles, go on believing. There are many signs in the world that God is healing our diseases and answering our prayers. Never doubt it.

However God works to heal us, my wife, Berny, has the right idea. If she doesn't feel well, she calls it what it is—sickness. It isn't normal, and it isn't permanent.

We all smile at the Christian layperson who was asked about his favorite verse of Scripture.

"It is found in many places in the Bible," he said. "It is, 'And it came to pass . . . ' Whatever happens, it didn't come to stay; it came to pass."

It is good to know that possibility.

As we look at the changing world scene, it is good to know about the eternal scent—the promise of a kingdom that will not be destroyed.

Even in our personal lives, we should not despair when our moods and our health seem to fluctuate. There is a kingdom within. We can live with temporary problems.

We are instructed to pray for healing. And so we pray believing, hoping, and trusting that God will honor his promises. Sometimes he answers those prayers with miraculous healings. Sometimes the healings are long and painful. At other times our prayers may seem unanswered. Those are the down times. You know how Lucy feels. We don't want down times. We don't want to see a friend or loved one who doesn't get well. How awful it feels when someone we love and have been praying for dies in spite of our concern!

What do we hang on to then? That is the crucial time when we must hang on to the kingdom dream within us. That is the time we remind ourselves that whether we see miracles or not, God's kingdom is in us. He still rules the

125

world and we can trust him however he answers our prayers.

3. Trust God to work out his kingdom plan in your life.

This is a story of a young man named Daniel as recounted in the Old Testament.

As it happens, while Daniel was serving the king he got in trouble, was put in prison, and was forgotten until the king had a dream that troubled him. God showed Daniel not only what the dream was, but what it meant.

> You looked, O king, and there before you stood a large statue—an enormous, dazzling statue, awesome in appearance. The head of this statue was made of pure gold, its chest and arms of silver, its belly and thighs of bronze, its legs of iron, its feet partly of iron and partly of baked clay. While you were watching, a rock was cut out, but not by human hands. It struck the statue on its feet of iron and clay and smashed them. Then the iron, the clay, the bronze, the silver and the gold were broken to pieces at the same time and became as the chaff on a threshing floor in the summer. The wind swept them away without leaving a trace. But the rock that struck the statue became a great mountain and filled the whole earth. . . .
>
> You, O king [the king of Babylon], are the king of kings. . . . After you, another kingdom will rise, inferior to yours. Next, a third kingdom. . . . Finally, there will be a fourth kingdom. . . . In the time of those kings, the God of heaven will set up a kingdom that will never be destroyed.
>
> —Daniel 2:31-40, 44, NIV

What do these strange images mean? The Bible itself gives an explanation. Daniel tells King Nebuchadnezzar that he is the "head of gold." He was overcome and his kingdom was succeeded by the Medo-Persian Empire. This in turn was overthrown by the Greek Empire. Under Alexander the Great it ruled the world. Alexander wept because there were no more worlds to conquer. The Roman Empire followed the Greek glory.

During the days of Rome's glory Jesus was born. He came proclaiming another kingdom—the kingdom of God. It was not made with human hands. It was—and is—a spiritual kingdom. I use the word *is* because Daniel's prophecy said that it would never be destroyed. It is alive and well now.

Since that is true, we must look for it. Jesus told us to seek it—in fact to seek it first. He also warned us that we could not see it with our natural eyes. "The kingdom of God does not come visibly, nor will people say 'Here it is' or 'There it is,' because the kingdom of God is within you" (Luke 17:21, NIV).

Can you imagine the comfort this prophecy brought to youthful Daniel as he tried to survive the temptations of dazzling Babylon? Riches and power could not tempt him. He knew (because of this vision) that the gold, silver, and bronze would mix with the dust. He was certain that God would have the last word.

God had let him look down the telescope of history to see that there truly would be a kingdom that would never be destroyed.

Daniel did not live to see all the other kingdoms rise and fall. From our vantage point in history we know that it happened; he could only believe. Daniel would not live to read the words of Thomas Gray written after the poet had visited a country cemetery:

The boast of heraldry, the pomp of power,
And all that beauty, all that wealth e'er gave,
Awaits alike the inevitable hour.
The paths of glory lead but to the grave.

While the kingdom of God is in the world today, it has not had its final victory. The time will come when all the kingdoms of the world will become the kingdoms of our God and of his Christ. This will come at the end of time.

We wait for that mind-stretching event, but we do not forget the present reality—the kingdom of God here and now.

127

It would be foolish to be so engrossed in the *prospects* of what will happen at the end of time that we forget the *possibilities* of kingdom living now.

Once we see eternal values, it is not hard for us to make temporary sacrifices. Once we have seen by faith the eventual victory God has planned, we should not be led astray by the political pied pipers of our day.

All of us are victims of others' schemes and designs—unless we are subject to the will of the King, the Lord of Lords.

A wonderful unity could be realized among Christians if they would proclaim excitedly that the Kingdom is forever.

In the world we will have struggles. In Christ there is victory. Believe in that possibility. It is a promise.

Churches are made up of people who have weaknesses—just like our own.

Chapter 10
Discovering God's Liberating Laws

Poor Linus. He is perfectly satisfied with being average. But Lucy won't let him off the hook. For a moment he throws her off base but you can trust Lucy to get her breath and begin hounding Linus again onward and upward to bigger and better things. That's what this chapter is all about. Once you join the Kingdom you have two choices: (1) you can stop right where you began and live there forever or (2) you can begin a lifelong spiritual pilgrimage that guarantees hard work, discovery, excitement, adventure, and danger.

Like Pilgrim in John Bunyan's *Pilgrim's Progress,* you now have the chance to begin a journey that will take you along the trails into the mysterious world of the kingdom of God inside you. God has wonderful surprises in store for those who refuse to settle in to being average. Don't give in to being average. Decide right now to spend your lifetime finding out God's will for your life and for the world in which you live.

There is a series of disciplines or *exercises* built into kingdom life that are guaranteed to help you grow. Like an exercise program in a gym, do these disciplines every day of your life and spiritual muscle will form that will get you through the troubled days ahead. Forget these disciplines, think you can make it without them, and your spiritual life is certain to shrivel up and die.

1. My Family Connections: the Discipline of Body Life.

The cell is at the heart of physical growth in our natural bodies. Cells make up our bodies. They live and die, eat and drink, and give birth to other cells. They are the basic unit of life. In the body of Christ, the local church is that basic unit. You cannot survive as a member of the Kingdom apart from being a part of a local cell. Attending worship, giving tithes and offerings, studying Sunday school or Bible study lessons, serving on work details—all of these activities of the local church can seem demanding or routine but in the long haul they are life-giving.

No local church is perfect. Every pastor or Sunday school teacher or lay leader is human. Churches are made up of human beings who have weaknesses like your own.

The writer of Hebrews made it perfectly clear that we are not to forsake coming together as a body (10:25). Get into the local cell of Christ's body. Take your place of responsibility. It is the most basic step of seeing growth in your own spiritual life, and as you grow the Body itself grows stronger.

2. Breathe New Air: the Discipline of Prayer.

You are a member of Christ's body, the Church. He is the head of that body. Prayer is the process of communicating with the head. Imagine what would happen to our human body if the brain wasn't in constant dialogue with each of the parts. Imagine what would happen if one of the parts got "off line" and simply did its own thing. The body would jerk out of control, wander off the path, trip and fall and be injured or paralyzed. But the body comes equipped for sending messages back and forth from the brain to every functioning organ. In our spiritual body prayer is the system that keeps communication open between God and his children. That's why the biblical author instructs each of us to "pray without ceasing" (1 Thess. 5:17).

If you've never prayed before, try reading the Lord's Prayer. You'll find it in Matthew, the first book of the New Testament (6:9-13). For the next few weeks simply read it at the beginning and the end of each day.

As you progress, add your own requests at each point in the prayer where they seem appropriate. Where Jesus instructed his disciples to pray, "Give us this day our daily bread" (v. 11), you could pause and add any requests you have for your provisions for that day. When our Lord says to pray, "Forgive us our debts, as we forgive our debtors" (v. 12), pause a moment and actually forgive those you need to forgive, confess your sins, and pray by name for those who have sinned against you.

You will find other beautiful prayers in your church hymnal or prayer book that you can pray as you are getting your own prayers together. Or you can simply begin by talking to God about anything and everything you feel like talking to him about.

133

Some people begin to keep a very careful list of those people or those issues for which they are praying. This makes it easier to remember the people in your life who need your prayers and the issues in the world for which you are concerned. Carry the list with you, and when you have a break during the day pray for them even if you have only seconds on the run.

Others enjoy turning off the car radio or the kitchen television so that they can tell God all the things for which they are thankful. Start out with the obvious—life, health, friends. Name each blessing as the chorus says, "Count them one by one and it will surprise you what the Lord has done."

You will find plenty of biblical instruction on prayer. Talk to your brothers and sisters about their prayer life. Read biographies on the great prayer warriors. Visit your Christian bookstore or church library and buy or check out books or pamphlets on prayer. Prayer is your lifeline to the Father. Keep it open.

3. *God Speaks Loudest in the Silence: the Discipline of Quietness.*

Charlie, you are like the rest of us. Our heads are buzzing with all the input we get from our friends and our enemies. (Sometimes it's hard to tell the difference.) Add to all the critical human voices echoing in our brain the noisy input of the television and radio and stereo (you can wear them now and have loud musical background for life) and it is no wonder we can no longer hear the still, small voice of God.

Count up all the times in the Gospels when eyewitnesses report that Jesus sneaked away from them to be alone. It takes going to a quiet place (even if that means simply locking oneself in a closet) to let the noise echoing in our brains gradually die down. Early in the morning Jesus went away to pray. Late in the evening they found him praying in the garden. At midday Jesus interrupted his journey to sit alone and pray.

Mastering the gift of silence is no easy task. Praying is not only speaking but listening. Until we learn to listen, until we can get past the current issues, problems, and ideas bouncing around in our brains and stay quiet and open to God, prayer will unfortunately be a one-way process.

Don't try too hard at first. Silence is scary. For one week try going to the same spot each day at about the same time just to be silent before God. Some people repeat a quiet phrase over and over again until the phrase replaces the noises in their heads. For example, "Lord I am you child. Speak your word to me." Others hum hymn tunes that relax them and help calm down their troubled minds. Others try

135

to get a picture of Jesus sitting beside them waiting to speak his words of comfort or confrontation. Others find a scenic place and stare out across the sea or a valley or down across a landscape. Some walk; some sit still. Some kneel; some sit with hands outstretched. Some close their eyes; some don't. Find your own best techniques, then master them.

4. Once over Lightly Is Not Enough: the Discipline of Meditation.

Once you've been able to drown out the distractions, even for a short period of time, and listen to God's voice in the silence, you are ready for some serious meditation. Most of us have never heard an audible voice when God speaks to us. (It would probably frighten us anyway.) So we take into the silence certain aids to help us focus our meditation, and often through these aids God speaks.

For example, the Bible is basic to meditation. Don't read a lot. This is not Bible study time. This is a time to read until what you read sparks a thought in you and then allow that thought to grow and develop prayerfully before God. Read one psalm and then think about it. Read a devotional booklet a few lines at a time until one line comes to life in your brain. Hymns are wonderful aids to devotion and meditation. You can meditate on one hymn for an entire week, phrase by phrase, verse by verse. Read and sing it quietly to yourself and let the meaning of each line grow and expand and be God's word to you for that day.

Don't worry if your mind wanders. That's what meditation is about. At first it will be hard to keep it moving in one direction. Work at it. When a thought interrupts your meditation, put it out of your mind and begin again. If that thought keeps returning, perhaps that's the idea God is leading you to think about. Robert Frost was asked the secret of his great poetry. He answered, "I have finally reached the place in my life when I can go into a woods thinking about one idea and come out the other end of the woods still intent on that same thought." Meditation is a skill. Work on it.

5. *You Never Run Out of Map: the Discipline of Bible Reading and Research.*

The Word of God is at the heart of our kingdom journey. Everybody knows that, but it is amazing to see how few of us do anything consistently about it. We have five or six translations on our shelves, but seldom do we read or study them faithfully.

Through the ages men and women of faith have discovered certain truths about the discipline of Bible study. First, find a place that is conducive to study. Second, go there. Equip that place with everything you'll need to study the Word: a translation that you enjoy and learn from; a pad and pencil; a concordance (a list of all the words in the Bible and where they are found); commentaries; study books about the Bible; and other appropriate aids. Third, set out a design for your study. There are wonderful plans to read the entire Bible through in two years or less. You may want to study one book, read all the books by one author, or study the Gospels to learn the life of Christ, followed by the Acts to experience the growth of that first-century body of believers. Fourth, try to read the Bible daily—at least a verse every day. Fifth, start memorizing your favorite passages. Sixth, keep a spiritual diary in which you write passages that have been particularly meaningful and what you've learned from them. Seventh, mark up your Bible. Write Scripture references in the margin that relate to the verse or verses you are studying. Underline basic themes with a colored pencil. The Bible should be a workbook, not simply an ornament on a shelf.

If you were to move to China you would be faced with some immediate decisions. How would you talk? How would you write? How would you read? You would obviously have to live by the laws of the land. You would be surrounded by the language of the land: Chinese. If you wanted to live happily in China you would have to learn both the language and the laws. Well, you have moved into the Kingdom and the Bible is the language and the law of the land.

Often, sincere Christians trying to understand the Bible become hopelessly lost as they try to fit all the pieces into a meaningful pattern. If they ask for help from their friends they find almost as many interpretations of what the Bible means as there are interpreters.

The last book in the Bible seems even more obscure than the others. Even so, it contains the key to understanding. The message is victory. God will have the final word. His kingdom will be victorious over all other kingdoms.

> The kingdom of this world has become the kingdom of our Lord and of his Christ. And he will reign forever and ever.
> —Revelation 11:15, NIV

Since this is the song we are going to sing in the future we should start practicing it now.

As we study the Bible we have good reason to be humble. Many questions remain unanswered. Although our understanding grows as we study, we never outgrow our need of faith. A study of history—and indeed a look at our own lives—will tell us that we have been mistaken about many things.

Snoopy encourages us to an intelligent humility. We all need it, Charlie Brown.

Humility, yes. Uncertainty? No. The certain future is that God will have the last word and those who have lived by the Word of the kingdom of God will see its glorious fulfillment.

The Kingdom invades the world now and conquers the world tomorrow. As we watch the rise and fall of earthly kingdoms we should not be dismayed. Poor nations will suddenly become rich and will turn in anger on those who have made them poor. Infant nations will flex their muscles and attack their aging neighbors. Kingdom will follow kingdom. Each change will threaten our peace of mind. It may threaten our peace and safety as well.

For the Christian this is a clear challenge to remain a citizen of a kingdom that cannot be destroyed. Whatever happens on the outside of us, we are protected and governed by the kingdom of God that is within us.

The conflicts of today should not distress us because God has, through his revealed word, the Bible, given us a glimpse at the tomorrow that awaits us. This is the greatest comfort.

Don't worry, Charlie. In spite of our misconceptions, our ignorance, and our fear, God's word to us will break through those words of Scripture and speak real comfort to our hearts. Master the discipline of Bible study and his Word will come to life in your heart. Ignore the Word and we risk missing the mark altogether.

A visitor from Mars who picked up a household magazine would be startled to see how much space is given to pictures of food and talk about food.

Chapter 11
Fasting: Let's Have Lunch and Talk about It

It is a good thing to have a few friends who will sharpen your mind and test your ideas. It is even better to have friends who are secure enough to challenge you when they think you are wrong. The best situation, however, is to have a few friends who are secure and available, as well as intelligent.

I have a friend like that. Dr. Perry Sperber is a dermatologist and a creative thinker. While we were neighbors in Florida we often found opportunity to talk about some of the ideas that were percolating in our minds. One day I called him.

"Perry, I am doing some research on fasting and I need to talk to a medical doctor about it. I think I understand some of the emotional and spiritual aspects of it. I believe it is a good thing and have practiced it for varying periods of time much of my adult life. But I need to know more about it. Do you have any information about what happens to the body during abstinence from food?"

"That is an interesting question," he said. "I really don't know much about it, since our church doesn't emphasize it. I would like to know more. Let's have lunch and talk about it."

As it turned out we did have lunch, and we did talk about it. Dr. Sperber finally sent to the University of Florida Medical School to get some information and research on fasting. More significant than our discussion, however, was his automatic response: "Let's have lunch and talk about it."

If a visitor from Mars were to pick up any household magazine he or she would be startled to see how much space is given to pictures of food and talk about food. Much of the remaining space would be filled with articles about losing the weight that is the evidence of our gluttony.

Between enormous food consumption and slow weight loss, life in America seems to be one long smorgasbord. Social engagements must be accompanied by food. Church suppers are fellowship times when food is carried in wrapped in foil and carried out under acres of sagging epidermis. Eating is a national pastime.

Even talk about fasting seems comfortable only in the presence of food. We do not easily let anything interfere with our mania for food. Denial seems almost like heresy.

Somewhere in our minds is a troubling memory. Jesus, the director of our lives and presumably our behavior, fasted—that is, he abstained from food. His great moments of triumph were preceded by fasting. On one occasion he fasted for forty days and nights.

Why? Is there power in fasting? Does it benefit our spiritual health? Does it help our emotional well-being? Could it yield even physical benefits? Is it a secret of power?

If it could do any of these things we ought to investigate it. At least we could have lunch and *talk* about it. Talking is not the same as fasting, but we are better at talking than we are at fasting. After all, we have to begin somewhere. Maybe if we talk about it long enough we will be able to harness the power of fasting to pull us away from the groaning snack bars of our mediocrity and obesity. It's worth a lunch to find out.

Staring up at me as I write this are the stark black letters from the title of a book called *Fasting Can Save Your Life*. As I study these words I ask myself, Can it really be true? It seems so simple to say that life does not consist of the things that we have but the things we are able to do without.

Health may be a matter not so much of what we eat but of what we don't eat. Unfortunately, most of us have the strange notion that if something is wrong with us we ought to take something for it. That something may be an aspirin or a bowl of chicken soup. As soon as infants are born, their well-meaning parents start cramming their mouths with as much food as they can hold.

Early in life we are told we must keep up our strength. We must eat. If eating alone would make us strong, the world would be full of Samsons. As it is, we are not Samsons.

On the back of Dr. Shelton's book about fasting is a strong statement: "Your body has remarkable recuperative powers when left alone." Other wisdom is contained in oft-quoted proverbs: "Half of what we eat keeps us alive; the other half keeps the doctors alive " or, "We dig our graves with our teeth." Another very appropriate one states, "The deadliest weapons in America are the knife, fork and spoon."

These words roll over our tongues but they seem to do little for our voracious taste buds. We simply keep on eating. Doctors tell us that obesity will shorten our lives by making us susceptible to heart disease, stroke, and diabetes. We are told that being overweight will give us a poor self-image. The more there is of us to think about the less we will think of ourselves.

How do we respond? We joke about our diets and keep on eating.

Why did Jesus fast? Why did he ask us to? Was he trying to tell us that there are indeed curative powers within the body that can heal us if we can give our body a rest from food? What did Jesus mean when he said, "I have meat to eat that you know not of"?

Are there lessons in nature about the restorative powers that are enhanced in our bodies when we go without food for a period of time?

A wild animal that is sick will retire to a cool, secluded spot and refuse to eat for days until it is well again. For some animals, fasting is part of the yearly routine.

Physicians know that fasting has merit; leaving the body alone so that it can heal itself is not new to them.

147

While I was a guest in the home of Dr. Jack Hutchinson I stubbed my toe on an iron bedpost. The toe turned a violent purple and became extremely sensitive. It appeared to be broken. Well, I thought, since I am in the home of an orthopedic surgeon I should get some advice on the proper care of my injured toe.

"Jack," I said, "I am not a medical man, but I have heard that the only cure for a broken toe is to leave it alone. Is that right?"

"If you had come to the office for an appointment I would have told you that, but I would have made it sound more impressive. I would have called the treatment 'professional neglect.' "

That incident reminds me of the words of a physician friend of mine who said, "Among doctors there is a saying, 'Encourage your patients to come to you at the first sign of illness. If they wait, they will probably get well but you won't get credit for the cure.' "

Of course, that is only partially true, but it does point out to us the marvelous restorative powers that are within us. If the body is not worked to death to process unnecessary food, it has opportunity to do its healing and restorative work.

Some fantastic physical benefits are derived from fasting. While they are not the only benefits, they are worth discussing. After all, the Bible tells us that our bodies are temples of the Holy Spirit and we aren't to defile them.

Following are some reasons for fasting.

1. *Weight Loss.* A fast is the simplest and most rewarding way to lose weight. Strangely enough, fasting is easier than dieting. When dieting, people are allowed limited amounts of food and are constantly encouraged to think about the things they cannot have. As soon as the diet is over, dieters have the urge to reward themselves for disciplined behavior. The natural thing is to eat the forbidden fruit.

While one is fasting, the first surprise is that after the first day the desire for food virtually vanishes. It becomes no hardship at all to watch other people stuff calories into their eager mouths. Experts testify that the proper time to end a diet of long duration—such as a fast for several weeks—is when hunger returns. This interestingly was true of Jesus' fast of forty days: "And when he had fasted forty days and forty nights, he was afterward an hungred" (Matt. 4:2). Only after the long abstinence from food did Jesus want it again.

It is not uncommon to lose from one to two pounds of body weight a day while fasting. If a prolonged fast is undertaken (and this should not be done without the advice of a physician), the weight loss slows down.

In March 1963 newspapers carried the story of a couple who survived a plane crash in northern British Columbia. After forty-nine days the couple was rescued in the wilderness in the dead of winter. Thirty days of this time were spent without food of any kind.

By means of a fire, a lean-to, and heavy clothes in which they wrapped themselves, the survivors managed to withstand the bitter cold. During the first four days after the crash they ate the four tins of sardines, two tins of fruit, and crackers they had on the plane. Twenty days after the crash the two ate their last food—two tubes of toothpaste. After that, melted snow became their diet for breakfast, lunch, and supper. They lived on water. They drank it three ways— hot, cold, and boiled—to relieve the monotony of their single-item menu: snow.

The young lady, who at the time of the crash was somewhat overweight, survived without danger to her health. She lost thirty pounds and her companion lost forty. Both were in good health when rescued.

2. *Bodily Compensation.* It is easy to see that all organs of the body cannot work equally hard all the time. When one is working another is waiting. For example, when someone is washing a load of clothes in the basement it is likely that the water in the upstairs shower will not run full force. When the body is consuming food the other organs cannot get their full share of energy.

Most of us know that after a full meal the natural desire is to sleep either physically or mentally. If we force ourselves to do hard work, the process of digestion is virtually suspended. Fasting makes possible the use of our energy in creative ways.

3. *Organic Rest.* When there is more to do we must work harder. This is also true of each organ of the body. The more food we take in, the harder our glands, heart, and digestive organs must work. When the intake slows down, these important parts of our body have a chance to rest. Respiration slows down and the nervous system has less work to do.

Rest is commanded in the Bible. The earth needs to rest. Is it surprising that the digestive system needs to rest as well?

4. *Elimination.* Most of us acknowledge that elimination is an important bodily function, but we act as though taking in food is most important. How wrong we are!

It has been proved that we can exist for as long as ninety days without food. The body cannot exist without elimination of some kind more than a few minutes.

Dr. J. H. Tilden of Denver, Colorado, says, "After fifty-five years of sojourning in the wilderness of medical therapeutics, I am forced to declare, without fear of successful contradiction, that fasting is the only reliable specific eliminant known to man."

Felix L. Oswald agrees with Dr. Tilden: "Fasting is the great system renovator. Three fast days a year will purify the blood and eradicate the poison-diathesis more effectively than bottles of purgative bitters."

Every business executive and every householder understands this principle. When you are doing a great deal of new business at the office or are having extra guests in your home, you cannot properly undertake major housecleaning. Only when you are freed from the pressures of new challenges can you find time to "clean out the closets."

Your body is like that.

While I do not profess to be a medical expert, these facts can be easily documented by a conversation with the best medical person you can find. I simply want to testify that a little fasting can't hurt you.

150

More important, however, than getting a new figure, an improved complexion, and better health are the emotional and spiritual values that come from fasting.

5. *Psychological and Spiritual Values of Fasting.* You will never forget your first fast. If you follow through with fasting one time, you will never let it be the last time. If you fail the first time, you will probably not try it again.

I can almost promise you that on the day you select for a fast someone will invite you to a delicious dinner. Your wife will choose that particular day to prepare your favorite meal. You will walk by someone's backyard while he or she is grilling steak. The aroma will drive you wild. I secretly suspect that the devil, as he is often pictured, uses his pitchfork for barbecues near the homes of fasting Christians.

You will be tempted. Though you think of yourself as a disciplined person you are not immune to the temptations of the flesh—including eating. Hunger will strike. The first hours are the hardest. They will remind you that the world is still a battlefield—a battlefield of competing kingdoms.

While you survive this battle you will have strange symptoms. You may have headaches, strange nervous reactions, or even nausea. You will think your health is being impaired by your fast. When you survive you will feel wonderful. You will feel like royalty because you will have taken charge of your life.

The first chapter in the book of will power is titled "Won't Power."

The spillover of this victory is amazing. When your friends tell you that they could not endure going without food for several days, you will feel an inner glow.

So far we have talked about the emotional and psychological values. There are more.

Jesus said when asked about the fasting of John the Baptist's disciples, "When the bridegroom shall be taken from them, . . . then shall [the children of the kingdom] fast" (Matt. 9:15).

Note that he did not say, "If you fast." He assumed that they would follow his example and fast.

151

On still another occasion Jesus told his disciples that their failure to cast the demon out of a young man was because "this kind [of miracle] cometh forth by nothing, but by prayer and fasting" (Mark 9:29).

In saying this did Jesus mean that we must bribe God to answer our prayers? Not at all. It simply means that fasting enables us to direct our faith and attention to the needed miracle. It works when nothing else does. Problems that arise at church suppers might be solved by fasting.

There may be many reasons why fasting is effective. I simply know that when I have a situation that will yield to no other kind of attack, fasting works. It unlocks doors that were otherwise closed.

But how do we fast?

Fasting is a deliberate abstinence from food for a specific period of time and for a specific reason. While the physical benefits of fasting are the same whether one has chosen to do it or has been forced to do it (as, for example, the couple who survived the plane crash in British Columbia), the spiritual benefits are not. For spiritual benefits to occur, the energy released by fasting must be directed toward some spiritual goal.

Some question exists in the mind of Bible students as to whether a fast should be kept secret. It seems to me that while we are warned against making a display of fasting by appearing emaciated or paranoid, we are not commanded to keep our fast a secret.

In fact, if you are fasting and simply tell your wife that you do not want to eat her cooking, you may have a new spiritual problem to pray about!

Again, looking at the example of Jesus and the others whose stories are told in the Bible, we see that fasting was not secret. If nobody knew about the fasts, how would we know? We are in fact told in the Old Testament to "proclaim a fast."

Will fasting hurt you?

Earlier in this chapter I referred to Dr. Perry Sperber, who agreed to have lunch and talk about fasting. As it turned out, he did write to the medical school from which he was graduated and obtain information about the effects of fasting on the human body. These findings have been duplicated in many other experiments.

The body, deprived of food from the outside, begins to consume food from the inside. First it eliminates the toxins and poisons that have been stored in the body, because the body itself has been too busy processing food to eliminate all the harmful things that have been stored away in it. After this preliminary cleansing it begins to consume the stored fat in the body.

This fat is stored not only in obvious places like the "spare tire" around the waist, but in the cumbersome upholstery of many other organs such as the kidneys and the liver. When all surplus fat is consumed the body begins to consume muscle tissues.

Only after all available tissue has been consumed does the body begin to consume the body organs themselves. The very last organ to be attacked is the brain. It is not likely, however, that anyone will do without food long enough to affect any body organs or the brain. The Great Physician is obviously very selective in deciding which parts of the body are most important.

Thinking about fasting? Have lunch with a friend and talk about it.

All the sermons in the world cannot compete with one friendly act of caring.

Chapter 12
How to Tell Your Friends and Keep Them Friends

Imagine Charlie Brown's predicament now that there are two counselors on his block, both offering solutions for life's deep dilemmas. Or worse yet, imagine your unbelieving neighbor's or friend's predicament in a world in which every street corner has someone offering the answers to life's most basic questions. Yet it is into just such a world that we are called to share our faith. "Go ye therefore, and teach all nations . . . whatsoever I have commanded you" (Matt. 28:19-20). This, according to eyewitness Matthew, was Jesus' last command to his disciples before his ascension. So sharing our faith becomes quite a priority. The problem is how we can share it most effectively.

1. *Before you share your faith remember these truths:*

First, we are not perfect, just forgiven.

We must never think that we have arrived. Every person with whom we share our faith must see us as fellow seekers after the kingdom of God.

Charlie, your humble spirit will draw people to you. Lucy's arrogance will turn people off. So it is in sharing our discoveries of the Kingdom. We are imperfect. What God has done for us in Christ makes us perfect in his sight. We are sinners. Christ's death and resurrection sets us free from the death we deserve. Then again, if you are honest with yourself you don't need me to tell you that you aren't perfect—do you?

Second, we are not good judges of who is perfect and who isn't perfect. "Judge not, that you be not judged," warns the Master. "For with the judgment you pronounce," he continues, "you will be judged" (Matt. 7:1-2). It is not our task to determine who is lost and who is found, who is directly in the middle of the road to heaven and who is wandering off that road to hell. Our task is simply to share our faith when and where it seems appropriate.

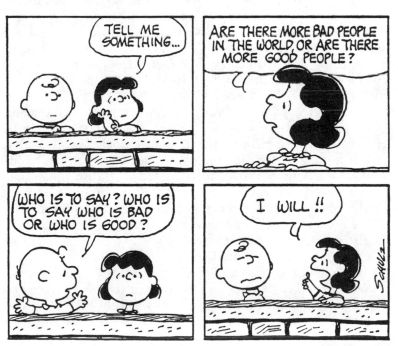

Third, remember we are not the Messiah, only his followers. Everyone needs a Messiah—a Savior. We are lost without him. But there is only one Messiah—Jesus. While we are told to share this good news with the whole world, we are warned about becoming little messiah's ourselves.

A messiah-complex can be deadly. It is the pathetic attempt to apply our home remedies to the ills of the world.

There is only one God, one King, one Lord of Lords. His plan is to enter our lives and work within us. He will reveal his word to us and in his own good time reveal that word to others.

2. While sharing your faith remember these truths:

First, you have to earn the right to be heard. "By your love will all men know that you are my disciples," Jesus told the Twelve—and they went out to change the world by loving it. "I have come into the world to save it, not to condemn it," Jesus said on another occasion. "What the World Needs Now Is Love Sweet Love." Remember that old song from the hit parade? Or what about "Don't Talk of Love, Show Me" from *My Fair Lady*? Lucy in her attempt to redeem Charlie Brown is destroying her right to be heard by him because she shows no love.

All the sermons in the world cannot compete with one act of caring. It may be a bowl of soup to a lonely, sick senior citizen, a surprise call to a friend who is lonely, a card with a gift of money to a struggling college student, a warm handshake to a neighbor who feels excluded during those first awkward days in a new home, or an offer to mow a lawn or haul a neighbor's trash when you have a pickup on the way. There are a million little ways and as many big ones to show Christ in your life. In such acts of love we earn the right to share our faith. Without that act of love we are, as Paul writes, "sounding brass and tinkling cymbals."

Second, tell is like it really is for you. Don't sweeten the truth. People want to know your downs, not just your ups, and your doubts, not just your acts of faith. Don't pretend to have all the answers when you don't. If they ask a question you can't answer, admit it and go looking for that answer for them. The Kingdom can stand our imperfection. The good news can bare up under the most intense inspection.

Third, don't oversimplify the truth. Avoid giving quick and easy answers to long-standing, difficult problems. People see through our simplistic solutions. They want to know where it has worked for us and where it has failed. They want to know the questions we have found answers to and the questions that still puzzle us. They want to hear truth as we have heard it. Trust them to figure out the rest. Then when you have told what you know, point them to the Scripture and assist them in their quest. But don't pretend the kingdom of God within us has too many easy answers.

3. *After sharing your faith remember these truths:*

First, be prepared for criticism. And be warned that sometimes criticism hurts. Right, Charlie Brown?

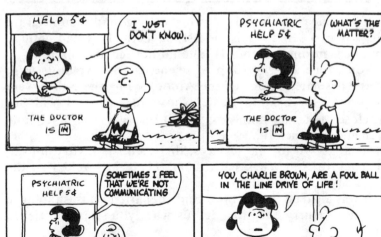

If you have not heard the story of Sagduluk you need to. He was in a sense a misunderstood hero. It is bad enough that he is misunderstood. He should not remain unknown.

Some time ago, a group of scientists and explorers went to the desolate regions of the Arctic. While there they were helped by an Eskimo guide whose real name I will not disclose. Let me simply say that he was well-liked and tremendously helpful.

As a reward for his services, the scientists invited him to go back to New York with them. There he could visit the great city and its sights.

It was a gala day when the guide departed on this fantastic journey. "Hurry back and tell us what you see," his friends said.

As the scientist suspected, the Eskimo guide was overwhelmed by the lights and action of New York City. It was almost more than he could believe—even though he was seeing it. "I can hardly wait to get back home to tell my friends what I have seen," he mused. "They will not believe it."

After a month among the world of tall buildings and bustling crowds he returned to the Arctic. As he expected, there was a great reception party. He was indeed a hero. He was filled with all kinds of stories—incredible stories.

"Do you know," he exclaimed, "that people in that land do not live as we do? They live in igloos piled on top of one another—as many as one hundred in a pile.

"They ride in strange *kayaks* that move under the earth. Each kayak holds hundreds of people. There are also kayaks that fly through the air."

As the newly returned hero told of the strange sights of New York City, his hearers began to nod meaningfully to each other. These stories were incredible. How could anyone believe them? In fact, after a tribal council they decided on a new name for their fellow tribesman: Sagduluk.

Sagduluk in the Eskimo language means liar.

Years did not change their attitude. Whenever Sagduluk would pass them they would nod sadly and remember the days when his conversations made sense—the days before his journey to a strange land.

Years later another guide had an opportunity to visit New York City as his reward for service to an exploring team. When he returned he was wiser than Sagduluk.

The welcoming group was treated to stories of New York City, but they were stories they could believe. "In New York," he said, "people live just as we do. They trade animal skins and live in little round ice houses. During the summer they fish in the rivers and dry the fish so they can have food for winter."

The guide was honored as a wise man.

The problem of Sagduluk is a common one. Jesus experienced it. After spending three years teaching extensively about the kingdom of God he was met with this question: "Lord, are you at this time going to restore the kingdom to Israel?" (Acts 1:6, NIV).

The Apostle Paul also shared Sagduluk's problem. In a

163

very amazing way he was able to be lifted out of himself so that he could see wonderful visions he called "the third heaven." I cannot describe what that was, because Paul himself could not describe it. Listen to his account:

> I know a man in Christ who fourteen years ago was caught up in the third heaven. Whether it was in the body or out of the body I do not know—God knows. And I know that this man—whether in the body or apart from the body I do not know, but God knows—was caught up to Paradise. He heard inexpressible things, things that man is not permitted to tell.
>
> —2 Corinthians 12:2-4, NIV

If indeed that man was Paul, as most scholars think, why could he not describe the things he had seen? Certainly no one was more eloquent than he.

The problem is that we cannot describe our spiritual journeys to earthbound people. There seems to be no vocabulary for it. Had he tried to tell people what he himself felt, they would have thought him insane.

Second, be prepared for a variety of responses. God has a wonderful sense of humor. He has managed to make us all unique. There are billions of us and not one is exactly like the other. Therefore, none of our responses will be the same. Enjoy the surprises you will find as people respond.

Charlie asked an honest question but got an answer he wasn't really prepared for. When you share your faith, get ready! The responses will vary.

In a day when we are beginning to understand the strange and wonderful relationships between the plants in the plant kingdom and the animals in the animal kingdom, it should not be difficult to understand diversity in the kingdom of God.

A casual look at the world of nature tells us that there are relationships that can be understood only by an infinite mind.

Crocodiles and birds live together. The bird eats the meat stuck in the crocodile's teeth and the crocodile allows it. It is the law of the kingdom of nature. A sparrow doesn't look like a crocodile or swim like one. He doesn't need to conform in order to belong.

Citizenship in the kingdom of heaven does not result in a kind of stereotyped march of the minds. It does not mean that each person's needs will be met by the same prepackaged theology. We will not look alike, think alike, or even completely understand each other. But we must love God in his perfecton and each other in our imperfections.

The goal of the gospel is that we will be "conformed to Christ," not that we will conform to each other. Jesus talked of this idea when he said, "The kingdom of heaven is like unto a net, that was cast into the sea, and gathered of every kind" (Matt. 13:47). Have you ever watched a net being hauled into an oceangoing boat? The sight will startle the most casual observer. Fish and other marine life defy description in their infinite variety of forms and colors. It is as though each one were trying to be as different as possible while living in the same ocean.

The conforming craze is a creation of humanity; it did not originate in the kingdom of God.

Third, once you have shared your faith, relax. God's Spirit will handle the rest. We want to push people into the Kingdom. Were you rushed? Did it help when people pushed you? Or were you led slowly and gently to truth by a loving, patient, courteous friend who respected your own integrity and honored God's timing?

We are all so unique that an infinite God must work out his purposes within us through the chemistry of those unique personalities. Outward conformity would never be real or lasting. Parents cannot push controls on us, nor can education or society—not even a highly evangelistic society.

We are routinely told that we are different. But we aren't told just how different. A recent educational journal states that if we could count the nerve connections in an average brain (these are what make up our experience and learning) we would have to put down a number 10 and add 5.6 million miles of zeros after it. Within that maze of connections are our feelings, our memories, our habits, and our experiences. No one looking at our brain from the outside can know exactly what we are feeling—or what we need to feel.

God can and he does, for he rules from within.

God's infinite mind will not invade people's lives against their wills. After we have shared our faith, after we have spoken his word as honestly as we can to them, we can relax and wait for his Spirit to do the rest.

Behold I stand at the door, and knock: if any man hear my voice, and open the door, I will come in to him and will sup with him, and he with me.

—Revelation 3:20

Share your faith. It is the next step on your wonderful kingdom journey. Enjoy!

This is *the* problem all of us face
when we try to change anything.

Chapter 13
Packing for a Long Journey

Randy and Sue were ready to build their new home—
their dream home. As they spread their plans before
the architect they said, "This is what we have decided we
want. Can you design it for us?"

"No problem."

"There is one more problem," Sue said. "We want to build
our new house out of the materials from the old house."

"Well," mused the architect, "that makes it a little more
complicated, but it can be done. It will take a little longer,
but it can be done."

"There is one more thing. We want to live in our old
house as long as we can while we build the new one."

"Now you have a real problem," replied the architect.

This is the problem all of us face when we try to change
anything. Even though we are not satisfied with things as
they are, we are not quite sure that we want to go through
all the hassle of living through change.

Even the suggestion that we ought to change is unwelcome.
Somehow we know inwardly that even the slightest change
can trigger a whole series of changes. We are up against a
brick wall—the wall of our own stubbornness.

Linus learned the lesson the hard way. He imagined that
all he would have to do to get a little more harmony in the
home would be to suggest in a kind tone that such a thing
was possible.

171

It is not that simple.

This is the old story of the Hebrew children and their attempt to escape brutalizing Egyptian captivity. While they felt the whips of their captors, they dreamed of freedom. Anything, it seemed, would be better than the agonizing labor. They prayed for a new life.

God heard their prayers, just as he will hear yours. It may be that he will not have to use all the spectacular miracles he used to pry the Hebrews free from their bondage, but he will do his best to get you safely through your kingdom journey. It will not be instantaneous or easy, but he will do it.

Were the Hebrews glad? Will you be? Listen to the amazing chant of the newly freed brickmakers:

In the desert the whole community grumbled against Moses and Aaron. The Israelites said to them, "If only we had died by the Lord's hand in Egypt! There we sat around pots of meat and ate all the food we wanted, but you have brought us out in this desert to starve this entire assembly to death.
—Exodus 16:3, NIV

Logic and reason could have told them how needful sacrifice is for progress, but what chance has logic or reason against our natural feelings? The dislike of being uprooted, of leaving a land we are not sure we are going to like, is painful. Becoming citizens of a new country, even the kingdom of God, is not without stress. How shall we deal with it?

1. The journey will be painful.

The prescription for freedom contains many things—and occasionally it is bitter. Progress is sometimes pain. If you reject the pain you may also reject the progress.

Dr. Paul Brand, who spent much of his life in India treating lepers, gives some fascinating insights into the nature of this dreaded disease. Most of us know that leprosy attacks the extremities of the body—the fingers, toes, nose, and ears—but we may not have understood that the disease itself does not eat away the tissue. It simply takes the feeling away from them. They lose their capacity for pain.

173

Since there is no sense of pain when a hand is laid on a hot stove or brushed roughly against a stone, the skin could be destroyed before any pain is felt. In primitive homes, rats or other vermin might eat away a leper's nose or ears and no attempt would be made to chase them away. Dr. Brand certainly knew this, but he had not realized how important a fact it was until he returned from a long trip to America.

As he lectured across the United States, Dr. Brand became exhausted even to the point of collapsing on the floor of the subway car in New York. Fortunately, he was able to drag himself to his hotel and once there try to rest. When he flew to England, the flight was crowded and he had no opportunity to walk around in the plane. The bus from the London airport was even more crowded and cramped. When he reached his home in London, he could scarcely stand. His legs would not support his body. They were without feeling.

While Dr. Brand worked among the lepers he had assured his helpers that leprosy was not contagious. If precautions were taken, he insisted, there was little chance that anyone would contract the disease from another person.

A horrible thought struck him. Is it possible, he wondered, that after all these years the disease had come to him? What if his hands that were accustomed to operating on the hands of others became only helpless stumps? What if he could not write or dress himself? What would his future be?

Taking a straight pin, Dr. Brand pushed it through the tough skin of his heel. A tiny spot of blood appeared. There was no pain.

Leprosy, he believed, the curse of millions, had come to him.

As he lay on his bed thinking of this, trying to imagine what changes there would be in his life because of it, he fell into a troubled but deep sleep.

When he awakened his first thought was to check once more to see if the disease was really attacking him. Nevously he took the straight pin again and pushed it through the touch skin of his heel. Even before the tiny spot of blood appeared he winced with pain. Pain! Blessed pain! No song was ever sweeter than that moment of pain. He was not a leper; he could feel.

What had happened was that the extreme exhaustion and crowding he experienced on his trip had affected the circulation in his legs, hence the numbness.

The pain of change in our lives is not pleasant, but it is better than death in a land of captivity. Changing the lordship of our lives will often make us wonder if we have done the right thing. Every minor change that comes in the rulership of our lives will make major changes in other areas of our lives. Sometimes the rest of us is slow to catch up.

2. *The journey will be slow.*

If you have ever noticed a deformity in your life, you may understand Mr. Schulz's insight. Peppermint Patty knows the agony of waiting.

The do-what-you-want pattern of living must be changed to the do-what-God-wants style of living. There is often a lag. Our character does not grow as rapidly as our ambition. This stretching is painful, but it is the price of growth.

Songwriter Bill Gaither illustrated this for me one day when he was talking of the aspiring musicians who ask for his help. "I really want to help them," he told me, "but I have learned that you do not help the butterfly when you open his cocoon for him. The struggle to get out of that confinement is precisely what forces the wings to become strong and beautiful. Too much haste and too much help destroys people."

God knows that. Maybe that's how Bill learned it.

Jesus faced the problem in his day. When he announced his kingdom his eager followers saw visions of shields and flashing swords. They were ready for instant change. They had no patience with the slow growth of character and grace within them. When they insisted that Jesus become their physical king, he had to remind them that his reign would be in their hearts.

Patrick Henry said, "Men will be governed by God or

they will be ruled by tyrants." Why is this so? If we will not respond to the inner rule, we will seek some authority figure from the outside who will promise us what we are not willing to pay for personally. We will seek someone who will do things for us instead of doing things within us.

Early in our marriage my wife, Berny, wanted to improve my rather drab taste in dress. Since I had lived a simple single life, traveling all over the world, my taste in clothes was very simple. I liked gray suits that didn't show soil. They never looked very good, but they didn't look very bad either. I needed only one pair of shoes. An extra pair would have been needless baggage.

Such simplicity would not do now that I was a married man. My wife decided that I needed another pair of shoes. These would be shoes worthy of a style-conscious wife.

I remember unwrapping the shoes she bought for me. I had seen them in the window of an exclusive store. They cost twenty-five dollors. This was almost as much as I paid for my suits in my single days. But since they were a gift of love I accepted them graciously, if somewhat reluctantly.

When I tried them on, I found them extremely uncomfortable. It seemed that there was something pressing against the arch of my foot. I could not escape the fact that I was wearing something new and uncomfortable.

When I returned to the store to ask if they were the right size the clerk measured my foot. Then he asked, "Mr. Berquist, do you know that you are flat-footed?"

"Yes, I'm afraid I am."

"That is the reason you need this arch support. The more you feel it, the more you need it."

These shoes could be a parable. The more painful it becomes for us to discover the kingdom of God in our lives, the more we need to discover it. The greater the tension between the former rule of self and the rule of the kingdom of God, the more desperately we need the pain and the tension.

It is true that God loves us just as he finds us, but he loves us too much to let us remain that way. To be changed may seem like more trouble than it is worth. But it isn't.

"The Kingdom does not come by observation," Jesus said. But it comes.

Even so, we understand the feeling of impatience. We all have experienced it.

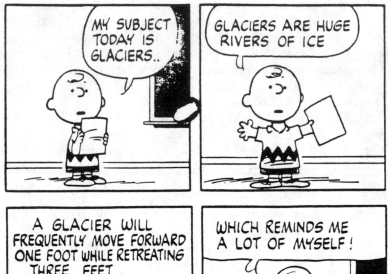

When we forget who we are, Charlie Brown, God remembers. And when we feel like quitting, he doesn't. He has been working on his plans for us for a long, long time.

It's great when we become aware of this.

3. *The journey will be wonderful.*

After all my talk about the "long" and "painful" kingdom journey that lies ahead, you must feel a bit like Charlie when Lucy gets through with him. Don't let that talk produce a dreariness in the air that depresses you. For the journey, though long and painful, leads to life everlasting. Imagine it. God loves you. He has invited you to be his co-worker in the redemption of the world. He has dreamed this dream for you since before he created the universe. He knows your name. He has plans for you. His Spirit will provide you the power to accomplish those plans. He has a purpose for you, and his Spirit will provide you the power to accomplish that purpose. He is in your life working out that plan right now. The Kingdom is within you. *The Doctor is in.* Enjoy the journey!